U.S. Supreme Court Transcript of Record Marine Nat Exchange Bank of Milwaukee v. Kalt-Zimmers Mfg Co

U.S. Supreme Court

Marine Nat Exchange Bank of Milwaukee v. Kalt-Zimmers Mfg Co
Transcript of Record / U.S. Supreme Court / 1934 / 148 / 293 U.S. 540 / 55 S.Ct. 85 / 79 L.Ed. 645 / 7-3-1934

U.S. Supreme Court Transcript of Record Marine Nat Exchange Bank of Milwaukee v. Kalt-Zimmers Mfg Co

Table of Contents

TRANSCRIPT OF RECORD

Supreme Court of the United States

OCTOBER TERM, 1934.

No. 148

MARINE NATIONAL EXCHANGE BANK OF MILWAUKEE AND WEST SIDE BANK, PETITIONERS,

vs.

KALT - ZIMMERS MANUFACTURING COMPANY AND M. H. GROSSMAN, TRUSTEE IN BANKRUPTCY.

ON WRIT OF CERTIORARI TO THE UNITED STATES CIRCUIT COURT OF APPEALS FOR THE SEVENTH CIRCUIT.

PETITION FOR CERTIORARI FILED JULY 3, 1934.

CERTIORARI GRANTED OCTOBER 8, 1934.

SUPREME COURT OF THE UNITED STATES

OCTOBER TERM, 1934

No. 148

MARINE NATIONAL EXCHANGE BANK OF MILWAUKEE AND WEST SIDE BANK, PETITIONERS,

vs.

KALT - ZIMMERS MANUFACTURING COMPANY AND M. H. GROSSMAN, TRUSTEE IN BANKRUPTCY.

ON WRIT OF CERTIORARI TO THE UNITED STATES CIRCUIT COURT OF APPEALS FOR THE SEVENTH CIRCUIT.

INDEX.

JUDD & DETWEILER (INC.), PRINTERS, WASHINGTON, D. C., OCTOBER 17, 1934.

—5514-C

For the Eastern District of Wisconsin

United States of America,   ⎫
Eastern District of Wisconsin. ⎬ ss.

At a stated term of the District Court of the United States of America, for the Eastern District of Wisconsin, begun and held according to law, at the City of Milwaukee, in said District, on the first Monday (being the 2nd day) of January, A. D. 1933, present the Honorable Ferdinand A. Geiger, Judge of said Court, presiding.

Among other the following proceedings were had, to-wit:

In the Matter of   ⎫
   Hackett, Hoff & Thierman, Inc., ⎬ In Bankruptcy.
           Bankrupt. ⎭

Be it remembered that on the 22nd day of March, A. D. 1933, a certificate for review of an order made by the Referee in re petitions of Marine National Exchange Bank of Milwaukee and West Side Bank, were filed as follows:

2   CERTIFICATE OF MILTON J. KNOBLOCK, Certi
   REFEREE, certifying the foregoing controversy to the   Re
Dist. Court of the U. S. for the East. Dist. of Wisconsin, filed as follows:

* * (Caption) * *

I, Milton J. Knoblock, one of the referees of said court in bankruptcy, do hereby certify that in the course of the proceedings in the above named cause before me the following matters arose pertinent to said proceedings:
First: that on the 26th day of September, A. D. 1931, the Marine National Exchange Bank, of Milwaukee, Wisconsin, filed its petitioner for authority to sell certain securities held by it to secure a collateral note of the above named bankrupt in accordance with the power contained in said note;
That thereafter and on the 22nd day of October, A. D. 1931,

Kalt-Zimmers Manufacturing Company, of Milwaukee, Wisconsin, made and filed its answer and cross petition to the petition of the said Marine National Exchange Bank, objecting to the granting of said authority to the said bank and praying that said collateral security be delivered to the trustee herein for the benefit and use of said Kalt-Zimmers Manufacturing Company;

that thereafter and on the 2nd day of November, A. D. 1931, the Trustee in Bankruptcy made and filed his answer to the cross petition of said Kalt-Zimmers Manufacturing Company herein;

that on the 3rd day of November, A. D. 1931, the said Marine National Exchange Bank, of Milwaukee, Wisconsin, made and filed its answer to the cross petition of said Kalt-Zimmers Manufacturing Company herein;

Second: that on or about the 22nd day of October, A. D. 1931, the West Side Bank, of Milwaukee, Wisconsin, made

3   and filed herein its petition for authority to sell certain securities held by it to secure a collateral note of the above named bankrupt in accordance with the power contained in said note;

that thereafter and on the 29th day of October, A. D. 1931, Kalt-Zimmers Manufacturing Company, of Milwaukee, Wissoncin, made and filed herein its answer and cross petition to the petition of the West Side Bank, objecting to the granting of said authority to said bank and praying that said collateral security be delivered to the trustee herein for the benefit and use of said Kalt-Zimmers Manufacturing Company;

that thereafter and on the 4th day of November, A. D. 1931, the West Side Bank made and filed herein its answer to the cross petition of the said Kalt-Zimmers Manufacturing Company.

Third: that on the 6th day of October, A. D. 1932, the referee gave notice by mail to all interested persons of a hearing upon said petitions of the said Marine National Exchange Bank and of the West Side Bank, and the cross petitions of the Kalt-Zimmers Manufacturing Company to each petition herein, and of the answer of the Trustee in Bankruptcy to said cross petitions; said hearing to be held in Room 400 of the Mitchell Building, Milwaukee, Wisconsin, on the 17th day of October, A. D. 1932.

Fourth: that thereafter and on the 17th day of October, A. D. 1932, and various adjourned dates, hearing was had upon said controversy, testimony was taken, exhibits filed, arguments of counsel heard, and briefs of counsel filed.

By stipulation and agreement by and between all parties concerned in said controversy, it was stipulated and agreed that the same questions being involved in the petition of both the Marine National Exchange Bank and the West Side Bank, and of the cross petitions of the Kalt-Zimmers Manufacturing Company to the petitions of each of said banks respectively, and of the answers to said cross petitions, that said matter be heard concurrently and in the same proceeding.

4 Fifth: that thereafter and on the 11th day of March, A. D. 1933, the referee made and entered his findings and order in said matter finding that the deposit of said bonds with the said Marine National Exchange Bank and with the said West Side Bank, of Milwaukee, Wisconsin, was not in violation of the Uniform Fiduciaries Act of Wisconsin; that the bonds in question were negotiable instruments; and that said bonds were complete and regular upon the face thereof; and that the bank in each instance became the holder before maturity without notice of dishonor, in good faith and for value, and without notice of deformity and defect in title, and in the usual course of business; and wherein the referee ordered that the cross petition of Kalt-Zimmers Manufacturing Company objecting to the authorization of the Marine National Exchange Bank to offer for sale and sell the bonds of the Kalt-Zimmers Manufacturing Company be denied and that the said Marine National Exchange Bank be authorized and empowered to offer for sale and sell said bonds; and wherein the referee ordered further that the cross petition of Kalt-Zimmers Manufacturing Company objecting to the authorization of the West Side Bank to offer for sale and sell the bonds of the Kalt-Zimmers Manufacturing Company be denied and that the said West Side Bank be authorized and empowered to offer for sale and sell said bonds;

Sixth: that on the 20th day of March, A. D. 1933, the referee received and filed the petition for review of the Kalt-Zimmers Manufacturing Company praying for a review of said order of the referee under date of March 11, 1933.

Seventh: that attached hereto and made a part hereof are the following portions of the referee's record in said matter;

(1) The petition of the Marine National Exchange Bank, of Milwaukee, Wisconsin, for authority to sell certain collateral securities.

(2) The answer and cross petition of Kalt-Zimmers Manu-

facturing Company objecting to the granting of authority to
sell collateral to the Marine National Exchange Bank.

5　　(3)　Answer of the Trustee in Bankruptcy to the cross
petition of Kalt-Zimmers Manufacturing Company regarding sale of collateral by Marine National Exchange Bank.

(4)　Answer of Marine National Exchange Bank to cross
petition of Kalt-Zimmers Manufacturing Company herein.

(5)　Petition of West Side Bank, of Milwaukee, Wisconsin,
for authority to sell certain collateral security held by it.

(6)　Cross petition of Kalt-Zimmers Manufacturing Company objecting to the granting of authority to sell collateral
to the West Side Bank.

(7)　Answer of the West Side Bank to the cross petition
of the Kalt-Zimmers Manufacturing Company objecting to
the sale of securities by West Side Bank.

(8)　Referee's notice of hearing and certificate of mail-
ing notices.

(9)　Referee's findings and order dated March 11, 1933,
upon the above controversy.

(10)　Petition of Kalt-Zimmers Manufacturing Company
for a review of the referee's order of March 11, 1933.

(11)　Bound volume of testimony including exhibits.

(12)　Exhibit B of West Side Bank, not included in bound
volume of testimony.

(13)　Exhibit 2 of Kalt-Zimmers Manufacturing Company not included in testimony.

(14)　Brief of counsel for Marine National Exchange
Bank.

(15)　Brief of counsel for West Side Bank.

(16)　Brief of counsel for Kalt-Zimmers Manufacturing
Company.

(17)　Reply brief of counsel for Kalt-Zimmers Manufacturing Company.

(18)　Transcript of decision of the Supreme Court for the
State of Wisconsin in re *Seth W. Pollard et al.,* v. *Marshall
& Ilsley Bank,* tendered by counsel for Marine National Ex-
change Bank.

(19)　Letter of Fish, Marshutz & Joffmann for Kalt-Zimmers Manufacturing Company in re *Pollard* v. *Marshall &
Ilsley Bank;*
all of said questions and the records relating thereto are
hereby certified to the judge for his opinion thereon.

Dated at Racine, Wisconsin, March 21, 1933.

(Signed Milton J. Knoblock,
Referee in Bankruptcy.

6 PETITION OF MARINE NATIONAL EXCHANGE BANK OF MILWAUKEE for authority to sell collateral security, filed as follows:

* * (Caption) * *

The Petition of Edward H. Williams of the City of Milwaukee, County of Milwaukee and State of Wisconsin, respectfully represents:

That he is a Vice-President of Marine National Exchange Bank of Milwaukee, a national banking corporation; that he makes this petition for and on behalf of said Marine National Exchange Bank of Milwaukee, being thereupon duly authorized.

That said Hackett, Hoff & Thiermann, Inc. was adjudicated a bankrupt on the 8th day of June, 1931, and that at such time said Hackett, Hoff & Thiermann, Inc. was indebted to said Marine National Exchange Bank of Milwaukee in the sum of Eighty-seven Thousand Seven Hundred Sixty-seven Dollars and Sixty-Two Cents ($87,767.62) together with interest from March 31, 1931, all in accordance with the tenor and effect of six (6) promissory notes, copies of which are hereto attached and marked ''Exhibit A.''

That as collateral and security for such indebtedness of said bankrupt to said Marine National Exchange Bank of Milwaukee, there were from time to time assigned, transferred and delivered to said Marine National Exchange Bank of Milwaukee sundry securities, and that at the time said Hackett, Hoff & Thiermann, Inc. was adjudicated a bankrupt, said Marine National Exchange Bank of Milwaukee held as collateral for such indebtedness certain securities; a list thereof is hereto attached and marked ''Exhibit B.''

That said Marine National Exchange Bank of Milwaukee, pursuant to the terms of said notes, is desirous of sell-
7 ing said securities at public sale, and with the right to be purchaser itself at such sale, and that it would be for the benefit of the estate of said bankrupt that said securities be sold pursuant to the power of sale contained in said notes.

Wherefore, your petitioner prays that said Marine National Exchange Bank of Milwaukee be authorized to make sale of the securities set forth in ''Exhibit B'' pursuant to the power contained in said notes.

Dated this 23rd day of September, A. D. 1931.

EDWARD H. WILLIAMS.

The foregoing petition having been duly filed and having come on for a hearing before me, of which hearing five (5) days' notice was given to M. H. Grossman, Trustee of the Estate of said bankrupt;

Now, after due hearing, it is ordered that said Marine National Exchange Bank of Milwaukee be and hereby is authorized upon five (5) days' notice to said trustee of the time and the place of sale to sell said securities held as collateral, and which securities are specified in the foregoing petition, keep an accurate account of the securities sold and the the price received therefor, and to whom sold, and said Marine National Exchange Bank of Milwaukee shall apply the proceeds of such sale: first, towards the expenses of such sale; second, towards the payment of the indebtedness of said bankrupt to said Marine National Exchange Bank of Milwaukee; and to pay the balance, if any, to said trustee.

Witness my hand this .... day of ...., A. D. 1931.

Referee in Bankruptcy.

8   EXHIBIT B.

Amount	Security
$ 5,500.00	Allen Bradley Company, Milwaukee, Wisconsin, First Mortgage Serial Gold Bonds, 5½%, due March 1, 1937.
20,000.00	Allen Bradley Company, Milwaukee, Wisconsin, First Mortgage, Serial Gold Bonds, 5½% due March 1, 1938.
10,000.00	The Argo Investment Company, Milwaukee, Wisconsin, Refunding First Mortgage, Serial Gold Bonds, 5½% due April 2, 1938.
10,000.00	Concordia Lutheran Church, Superior, Wisconsin, First and Refunding, First Mortgage Serial Gold Bonds, 6%, due August 1, 1940.
1,000.00	Harmony Realty Company, Milwaukee, Wisconsin, First Mortgage, Serial Gold Bonds, 6% due December 1, 1938.
6,000.00	Kalt-Zimmers Manufacturing Company, Milwaukee, Wisconsin, Refunding First Mortgage, Serial Gold Bonds, 6%, due August 15, 1939.
500.00	Kosciuszko Furniture Company Building, Refunding First Mortgage Serial Gold Bond, 6%, due March 1, 1939.

1,000.00	Manufacturers Sites Corporation, Milwaukee, Wisconsin, Refunding First Mortgage, Serial Gold Bonds, 6% due October 1, 1931.
1,000.00	Manufacturers Sites Corporation, Milwaukee, Wisconsin, Refunding First Mortgage, Serial Gold Bond, 6% due October 1, 1941.
1,000.00	Manufacturers Sites Corporation, Milwaukee, Wisconsin, Refunding First Mortgage Serial Gold Bond, 6% due October 1, 1942.
7,000.00	Manufacturers Sites Corporation, Milwaukee, Wisconsin, Refunding First Mortgage, Serial Gold Bond, 6% due October 1, 1943.
500.00	Milwaukee Novelty Dye Works, Milwaukee, Wisconsin, First Mortgage Serial Gold Bonds, 6% due July 15, 1940.
1,000.00	Northern Finance Company, Green Bay, Wisconsin, 6% First Mortgage Serial Gold Bond due November 1, 1939.
2,000.00	Northern Finance Company, Green Bay, Wisconsin, 6% First Mortgage Serial Gold Bond due November 1, 1941.
1,000.00	Northern Finance Company, Green Bay, Wisconsin, 6% First Mortgage Serial Gold Bond due November 1, 1942.
500.00	Republic Investment Company, Milwaukee, Wisconsin First Mortgage, 6½% Gold Bonds, due July 1, 1931.
1,000.00	Republic Investment Company, Milwaukee, Wisconsin, Refunding First Mortgage Leasehold, Serial Gold Bonds, 6% due February 1, 1937.
1,000.00	Republic Investment Company, Milwaukee, Wisconsin, Refunding First Mortgage Leasehold, Serial Gold Bond, 6% due February 1, 1939.
$ 2,000.00	St. Ignatius Congregation, Milwaukee, Wisconsin, Refunding Second Mortgage Gold Bonds, 6% due April 15, 1937.
1,500.00	St. Josephs Hospital, Hartford, Wisconsin, Second Mortgage Serial Gold Bond, 5½%, due June 1, 1935.
1,000.00	St. Josephs Hospital, Hartford, Wisconsin, Second Mortgage Serial Gold Bond, 5½% due June 1, 1936.
1,000.00	St. Josephs Hospital, Hartford, Wisconsin, Second Mortgage Serial Gold Bond, 5½% due June 1, 1940.

9

4,000.00	St. Josephs Hospital, Hartford, Wisconsin, Second Mortgage Serial Gold Bond, 5½% due June 1, 1941.
3,000.00	St. Josephs Hospital, Hartford, Wisconsin, Second Mortgage Serial Gold Bond, 5½% due June 1, 1942.
500.00	St. Josephs Hospital, Hartford, Wisconsin, Second Mortgage Serial Gold Bond, 5½% due June 1, 1943.
1,000.00	St. Mary's Mothers and Infants Home, Green Bay, Wisconsin, Refunding First Mortgage, Serial Gold Bond, 5% due March 1, 1934.
1,000.00	St. Mary's Mothers and Infants Home, Green Bay, Wisconsin, Refunding First Mortgage, Serial Gold Bond, 5% due March 1, 1935.
6,500.00	St. Mary's Mothers and Infants Home, Green Bay, Wisconsin, Refunding First Mortgage, Serial Gold Bond, 5% due September 1, 1937.
6,000.00	Shafrin, Schmitz & Company, Milwaukee, Wisconsin, Refunding First Mortgage, Serial Gold Bond, 6% due September 15, 1940.
1,000.00	Simpson Methodist Episcopal Church, Milwaukee, Wisconsin, Refunding First Mortgage, 5½% Serial Gold Bond, due September 1, 1937.

Endorsed: "Filed Sept. 26, 1931   Milton J. Knoblock, Referee."

10   ANSWER AND CROSS-PETITION OF KALT-ZIMMERS MANUFACTURING CO. to petition of the Marine National Exchange Bank of Milwaukee, filed as follows:

* * (Caption) * *

And now comes Kalt-Zimmers Manufacturing Company, of the city of Milwaukee, state of Wisconsin, and, in answer to the petition of the Marine National Exchange Bank filed in this matter and dated September 23, 1931, admits, denies, and alleges, as follows:

1.   Admits that the Marine National Exchange Bank of Milwaukee is a banking corporation located in the city of Milwaukee, in the state of Wisconsin.

2.   Admits that Hackett, Hoff & Thiermann, Inc. was duly adjudicated a bankrupt on the 8th day of June, 1931.

3. It denies knowledge or information sufficient to form a belief as to whether or not Hackett, Hoff & Thiermann, Inc. was indebted to the said Marine National Exchange Bank of Milwaukee on said date, as set forth in the petition herein referred to, and thereunto puts the petitioner to its proof.

4. Admits that said Hackett, Hoff & Thiermann, Inc. attempted to pledge with said bank certain security as collateral to its indebtedness to said Marine National Exchange Bank,

11   but denies knowledge or information sufficient to form a belief as to what collateral was attempted to be pledged and to secure what debts the same were pledged, and thereunto puts the petitioner to its proof.

5. This answering respondent, in further answer to the said petition of the said Marine National Exchange Bank herein referred to, and by way of cross-petition thereto, alleges:

(a)   That it is a corporation duly organized and existing under and by virtue of the laws of the state of Wisconsin, located at Milwaukee, Wisconsin.

(b)   That on or about the 15th day of August, A. D. 1929, it made, executed, and delivered to Hackett, Hoff & Thiermann, Inc., a corporation of the state of Wisconsin, as trustee, certain of its property located in the city of Milwaukee, it conveyed to said Hackett, Hoff & Thiermann, Inc., as trustee, a certain of its property located in the city of Milwaukee, as security for its Six Per Cent. Refunding First Mortgage Serial Gold Bonds of a total principal sum of One hundred Fifteen thousand dollars ($115,000.00); that all of said bonds were duly executed by this answering respondent and duly certified by Hackett, Hoff & Thiermann, Inc., as trustee, as provided for in said deed of trust.

That said bonds issued pursuant to the terms of said trust mortgage contain, among other things, the following provision:

*   *   *   ''Said bonds are issued under and secured by a mortgage or deed of trust of even date herewith, duly made, acknowledged and delivered by said Kalt-Zimmers Manufacturing Company to Hackett, Hoff & Thiermann, Incorporated,

12   trustee, to which deed of trust reference is hereby made with the same effect as though recited at length herein,

for the description of the property mortgaged, the nature and extent of the security, the rights of the holders of the bonds, and the terms and conditions upon which the said bonds are issued, held and secured, and may, before their fixed maturities, be declared at once due and payable, and the manner of prepayment before maturity.''

(c) This answering respondent further shows to the court that the said trust deed referred to in said bonds contains the following provisions:

"Whereas, there is an encumbrance existing against the premises above described, evidenced by a mortgage or deed of trust in the principal sum of Fifty-five Thousand Dollars ($55,000.00), dated the first day of January, 1923, recorded in the office of the Register of Deeds of Milwaukee county, Wisconsin, on the second day of January, 1923, in Volume 1087 of Mortgages, page 36, Document No. 1184879, and on which trust deed or mortgage there is unpaid a balance of principal of Thirty-five Thousand Dollars ($35,000.00);

"Now, Therefore, It Is Agreed, that said Trustee first set aside and hold a sufficient number of bonds or the proceeds of a sufficient number of bonds to fully pay and satisfy, as soon as it can be done, the above mortgage in the principal sum of Fifty-five Thousand Dollars ($55000.00); and after so setting aside such sufficient number of bonds or the proceeds of a sufficient number of bonds for the above purpose of paying and satisfying the above mortgage, the pro-
13 ceeds of the balance and remainder of said bonds shall then be paid out in liquidation of the cost of the contemplated building in course of erection or to be erected on said premises, upon architect's certificates issued from time to time for completed construction to date of such architect's certificates, and if any balance remains after the completion and full payment of said building, the balance is then to be at the disposal of the party of the first part.

This answering respondent further shows that said mortgage of Fifty-five thousand dollars ($55,000.00), referred to in said trust deed, and the bonds secured thereby, were never paid and said mortgage was never satisfied.

(d) This answering respondent further shows that none of the said Six Per Cent. Refunding First Mortgage bonds was ever sold by or for this respondent, that respondent never received any consideration therefor, and that the said Hackett, Hoff & Thiermann, Inc., gained possession thereof only as trustee under the said deed of trust, and that Six thousand dollars ($6,000.00) par value of the said Six Per Cent. Refunding First Mortgage bonds secured by said trust indenture dated August 15, 1929, and issued by this answering respondent, are now in the possession of the petitioner, Marine National Exchange Bank, under claim of title thereto as set forth in its petition herein referred to, and alleges that said Marine National Exchange Bank has no right, title or interest in and to the said Six thousand dollars ($6,000.00) par value of bonds issued by this answering respondent as herein set forth.

(e) This answering respondent further alleges that M. H. Grossman has been and now is the duly elected qualified,
14 and acting Trustee in Bankruptcy of Hackett, Hoff & Thiermann, Inc.

Wherefore, This answering respondent prays that the bonds issued by it dated on or about August 15, 1929, of the aggregate principal amount of Six thousand dollars ($6,000.00) and now held by the petitioner, Marine National Exchange Bank, be ordered to be delivered to it by said Marine National Exchange Bank, or that said bonds be delivered to M. H. Grossman as trustee in bankruptcy for said Hackett, Hoff & Thiermann, Inc., for the benefit and to the use of this answering respondent.

KALT-ZIMMERS MANUFACTURING COMPANY

By JOHN B. CASPER

Sec'y.

FISK, MARSHUTZ & HOFFMAN,
    Attorneys for Kalt-Zimmers Manu-
    facturing Company.

State of Wisconsin, }
Milwaukee County. } ss.

JOHN B. CASPER, being first duly sworn, on oath deposes and says that he is the secretary of the above and foregoing corporation, Kalt-Zimmers Manufacturing Company; that he has read the above and foregoing answer and cross-petition, and that the same is true of his own knowledge, except as to such matters therein stated on information and belief, and as to them he believes it to be true; that he makes this verification for and on behalf of said corporation and is authorized to do so.

JOHN B. CASPER.

Subscribed and sworn to before me this 21st day of October, A. D. 1931.

(Seal)

FLORENCE BUCK

Notary Public, Milwaukee Co., Wis.

My commission expires June 30, 1935.

Endorsed: "Filed Oct. 22, 1931 Milton J. Knoblock, Referee."

15   ANSWER OF MARINE NAT'L EXCHANGE BANK
OF MILWAUKEE to cross-petition of the Kalt-Zimmers Manufacturing Company, filed as follows:

* * (Caption) * *

The answer of the petitioner, Marine National Exchange Bank of Milwaukee, to the cross-petition herein filed on behalf of Kalt-Zimmers Manufacturing Company respectfully shows to the court:

One. This petitioner admits the allegations of paragraph 5(a) of said cross-petition.

Two. This petitioner admits the allegations of paragraph 5(b) of said cross-petition, and this petitioner attaches hereto a photostatic copy of one of said bonds, the others of said bonds being of like form and tenor, except as to number and amount, and such photostatic copy hereto attached is marked "Exhibit A" and made a part hereof as if fully set forth herein.

Three. This petitioner admits that said trust deed referred to in said bonds contains the provisions set forth in paragraph 5(c) of said cross-petition. This petitioner has no knowledge or information that said mortgage of Fifty-five Thousand Dollars ($55,000) referred to in said trust deed or the bonds secured thereby were never paid or said mortgage was never satisfied, and demands strict proof thereof.

Four. This petitioner has no knowledge or information that none of said six per cent. (6%) refunding first mortgage bonds were vere sold by or for said Kalt-Zimmers Manufacturing Company, or that said Kalt-Zimmers Manufacturing Company never received any consideration therefor, and demands strict proof thereof; denies that said Hackett,
16 Hoff & Thiermann, Inc. gained possession of said bonds only as trustee under the said deed of trust; admits that Six Thousand Dollars ($6000) par value of said six per cent. (6%) refunding first mortgage bonds secured by said trust indenture dated August 15, 1929, and issued by said Kalt-Zimmers Manufacturing Company are now in the possession of this petitioner as set forth in its petition heretofore filed; denies that this petitioner has no right, title or interest in or to said Six Thousand Dollars ($6000) par value of bonds issued by said Kalt-Zimmers Manufacturing Company. This petitioner alleges that said bonds were complete and regular upon their face; that this petitioner became the holder there-

of before the same were overdue; that this petitioner received said bonds in good faith and for value; that at the time the same were negotiated to this petitioner, this petitioner had no notice of any infirmity in the nstrument, or defect in the title of said Hackett, Hoff & Thiermann, Inc., Bankrupt, and that this petitioner took said bonds in the usual course of business; and this petitioner alleges that said bonds are negotiable instruments, and this petitioner is the bona fide holder for value thereof. This petitioner alleges that said Kalt-Zimmers Manufacturing Company delivered said bonds to said Hackett, Hoff & Thiermann, Inc., Bankrupt, and clothed said Hackett, Hoff & Thiermann, Inc. with apparent authority to transfer the same, and that said Hackett, Hoff & Thiermann, Inc. within the apparent scope of its authority, did transfer said bonds to this petitioner for value without notice of any limitations of its authority.

Five. This petitioner admits the allegations contained in paragraph 5(e) of said cross-petition.

Wherefore, this petitioner prays that said cross-petition be dismissed with costs.

MARINE NATIONAL EXCHANGE BANK OF MILWAUKEE
By EDWARD H. WILLIAMS
Vice-President

KAUMHEIMER & KAUMHEIMER and
DOUGLASS VAN DYKE,
    Attorneys for Marine National Exchange
    Bank of Milwaukee.

17   State of Wisconsin }
      Milwaukee County } ss.

EDWARD H. WILLIAMS, being first duly sworn, on oath deposes and says that he is a Vice-President of the Marine National Exchange Bank of Milwaukee, the petitioner in this matter. That he has read the foregoing answer to the cross-petition of Kalt-Zimmers Manufacturing Company and knows the contents thereof, and that the same is true to his own knowledge, except as to those matters therein stated to be on information and belief, and as to those matters he believes it to be true.

EDWARD H. WILLIAMS (Signed)

Subscribed and sworn to before me this 30 day of October, A. D. 1931.

CARL ANDERSON (Signed)
Notary Public, Milwaukee County, Wis.

(Seal)

My Comm. expires: Feb. 28, 1932.

Endorsed: Filed Nov. 5, 1931 Milton J. Knoblock, Referee.''

18 ANSWER OF M. H. GROSSMAN, TRUSTEE, to the Cross-petition of Kalt-Zimmers Manufacturing Co., filed as follows:

IN THE DISTRICT COURT OF THE UNITED STATES

For the Eastern District of Wisconsin.

In the Matter of
Hackett, Hoff & Thiermann, } In Bankruptcy
Bankrupt.

Now comes M. H. Grossman, trustee of Hackett, Hoff & Thiermann, Inc., bankrupt, and for answer to the cross petition of Kalt-Zimmers Manufacturing Company alleges as follows:

Admits the allegations in paragraph 5(a), (b) and (c), contained in the cross petition of Kalt-Zimmers Manufacturing Company.

Further answering, and in answer to the allegations contained in paragraph 5 (d), the trustee alleges as follows:

Admits that Six Thousand Dollars ($6,000) par value of the bonds issued by the cross-petitioner are now in the possession of Marine National Exchange Bank, and alleges that in accordance with the trust agreement Kalt-Zimmers Manufacturing Company issued and delivered to Hackett, Hoff & Thiermann, Inc., bankrupt, the bonds as set forth in said trust agreement, and that subsequent to the receipt of said bonds, Ninety Thousand Dollars ($90,000) par value of the said bonds were sold pursuant to the terms of said trust and that Fourteen Thousand Five Hundred Dollars ($14,500) par value of said bonds were pledged as security for various loans made to Hackett, Hoff & Thiermann, Inc., bankrupt, Four Thousand Dollars ($4000.00) were pledged by Max L. Thiermann, deceased, to secure certain loans made to said deceased, and that Six Thousand Five Hundred Dollars ($6,500) par value of said bonds are still retained by and in the possession of the trustee of said Hackett, Hoff & Thiermann, Inc., bankrupt.

Wherefore, the trustee prays that the cross-petition of Kalt-Zimmers Manufacturing Company be dismissed.

BENDER, TRUMP, McINTYRE & FREEMAN,
Attorneys for Trustee.

19   State of Wisconsin } ss.
Milwaukee County

M. H. GROSSMANN, being first duly sworn, on oath deposes and says that he is the trustee of Hackett, Hoff & Thiermann, Inc., bankrupt; that he has read the above and foregoing answer to the cross petition of Kalt-Zimmers Manufacturing Company and knows the contents thereof, and that the same is true of his own knowledge, except as to matters therein stated on information and belief and as to those matters he believes it to be true.

M. H. GROSSMANN (Signed)

Subscribed and sworn to before me this 31st day of October, 1931.

RONOLD A. DRESCHLER (Signed)
(Seal)   *Notary Public, Milwaukee County,*
Wisconsin.

My Commission expires March 11, 1934.

20   PETITION OF WEST SIDE BANK for authority to sell collateral security, filed as follows:

* *   (Caption)   * *

To: Hon. Milton C. Knoblock, Referee in Bankruptcy.

The petitioner of the West Side Bank, a banking corporation, duly organized, existing and doing business under and by virtue of the laws of the State of Wisconsin, and located in the City of Milwaukee, Wisconsin, respectively represents:

That the above named Hackett, Hoff & Thiermann, Inc. was duly adjudicated bankrupt in and by the above named court on the 8th day of June, 1931. That said bankrupt was at said time indebted to said petitioner in the sum of Seventy-two Thousand Nineteen and 80/100 Dollars ($72,019.80) upon those certain promissory notes hereinafter mentioned theretofore duly executed and delivered to said petitioner by said Hackett, Hoff & Thiermann, Inc. That the amounts so due said petitioner upon said several promissory notes are as follows, to-wit:

Upon that certain promissory note executed and delivered by said bankrupt to said petitioner on the 6th day of March, 1931, in the principal sum of $10,000.00 payable 60 days after date together with interest at the rate of 6½% per annum, in the sum of $9015.47 as principal together with interest thereon at the rate of 6½% per annum from the 5th day of May, 1931, said interest amounting to the sum of $27.67 on the 22nd day of May, 1931.

Upon that certain promissory note executed and delivered by said bankrupt to said petitioner on the 31st day of March, 1931, in the principal sum of $10,000.00 payable 60 days after date together with interest at the rate of 6½% per annum, in the sum of $10,000.00 as principal together with interest thereon at the rate of 6½% per annum from the 31st day of March, 1931, said interest amounting to the sum of $93.89 on the 22nd day of May, 1931.

21   Upon that certain promissory note executed and delivered by said bankrupt to said petitioner on the 18th day of April, 1931, in the principal sum of $20,000.00 payable 30 days after date together with interest at the rate of 6½% per annum, in the sum of $20,000.00 as principal together with interest thereon at the rate of 6½% per annum from the 18th day of April, 1931, said interest amounting to the sum of $122.77 on the 22nd day of May, 1931.

Upon that certain promissory note executed and delivered by said bankrupt to said petitioner on the 4th day of April, 1931, in the principal sum of $27,500.00 payable 60 days after date together with interest at the rate of 6½% per annum, in the sum of $27,500.00 as principal together with interest thereon at the rate of 6½% per annum from the 4th day of April, 1931, said interest amounting to the sum of $238.33 on the 22nd day of May, 1931.

Upon that certain promissory note executed and delivered by said bankrupt to said petitioner on the 28th day of April, 1931, in the principal sum of $5000.00 payable 30 days after date together with interest at the rate of 6½% per annum, in the sum of $5000.00 as principal together with interest thereon at the rate of 6½% per annum from the 28th day of April, 1931, said interest amounting to the sum of $21.67 on the 22nd day of May, 1931.

That true and correct copies of said promissory notes are hereto attached, made a part hereof and marked "Exhibit 1."

That as collateral security for the payment of said indebtedness, the said bankrupt had from time to time pledged with your petitioner certain bonds under and pursuant to the terms and conditions of the pledge agreement contained in said notes and at the time of the adjudication of bankrupt herein said petitioner held as collateral security for the payment of the indebtedness due upon said notes those certain bonds described upon "Exhibit 2" hereto annexed and made a part hereof. That said petitioner desires to sell said bonds so pledged as collateral security for the payment of said notes pursuant to the terms and with the privileges contained in the pledge agreements in said notes.

Wherefore said petitioner prays that it be authorized to make sale of said bonds hereinbefore referred to pursuant to the power of sale contained in said notes.

Dated, Milwaukee, Wisconsin, October ...., 1931.

WEST SIDE BANK, *Petitioner,*
By CHARLES J. KUHNMUENCH,
Its President.

22 State of Wisconsin }
    Milwaukee County } ss.

CHARLES J. KUHNMUENCH, being first duly sworn on oath, deposes and says that he is an officer, to-wit, the President of the West Side Bank, the petitioner in the foregoing matter; that he makes this verification on its behalf and is duly authorized so to do; that he has read the foregoing petition and knows the contents thereof and that the same is true to his own knowledge except as to matters therein stated on information and belief and as to those matters he believes it to be true; that the reason this verification is not made by petitioner is that petitioner is a corporation and deponent is such officer thereof and is acquainted with the facts; that the sources of his information and the grounds of his belief are the records and files of said corporation and statements made to him by officers and agents of petitioner corporation in the regular course of their duties.

CHARLES J. KUHNMUENCH.

Subscribed and sworn to before me this .... day of ...., 1931.

ADA VAN RHIENEN,
Notary Public, Milwaukee County,
Wisconsin.

My Commission expires: Oct. 22, 1933.

$2000.00 par value Allen Bradley Company first mortgage bonds Nos. 358-502-503-504 of the par value of $500.00 each.

$8500.00 par value Kalt-Zimmers Mfg. Co. Refunding First Mortgage bonds Nos. 94-95-96-110-128-129-130 of the par value of $500.00 each and Nos. 62-66-72-73-74 of the par value of $1000.00 each.

$5000.00 par value Concordia Lutheran Church, Superior, Wis. 1st and refunding 1st mortgage bonds Nos. 147-148-149-150-151 of the par value of $1000.00 each.

$7000.00 par value St. Alexander Congregation, Milwaukee, Wis. refunding 1st mortgage Nos. 114 to 120 incl. of the par value of $1000.00 each.

$5000.00 par value Shafrin, Schmitz & Company, Milwaukee refunding 1st mortgage bonds Nos. 53 to 57 incl. of the par value of $1000.00 each.

$5000.00 par value Loyal Order of Moose, Kenosha Lodge No. 286 Refunding 1st mortgage bonds Nos. 121 to 125 incl. of the par value of $1000.00 each.

$1000.00 par value Manufacturers Sites Corporation, Milwaukee, bond No. 83 refunding 1st mortgage.

$6000.00 par value South Baptist Church, Milwaukee, Wis. Refunding 1st mortgage bonds Nos. 70 to 75 incl. of the par value of $1000.00 each.

$5000.00 par value St. Ignatius Congregation, Milwaukee, Wis. refunding second mortgage bonds Nos. 36-40 incl. and 81 to 85 incl. of the par value of $500.00 each.

$5000.00 par value Sacred Heart Congregation, Milwaukee, Wis. Refunding 1st mortgage bonds Nos. 69 to 78 incl. of the par value of $500.00 each.

$7000.00 par value Grace Manor (Monroe Realty Co. Inc.) 1st mortgage bonds Nos. 145 to 158 incl. of the par value of $500.00 each.

$16000.00 par value The Argo Investment Co., Milwaukee, Wis. Refunding 1st mortgage bonds Nos. 395 to 418 incl. and 292 to 297 incl. and 354-269 of the par value of $500.00 each.

$1000.00 par value St. Josephs Hospital, Hartford, Wis. Second mortgage bonds Nos. 19 and 20 of the par value of $500.00 each.

$2000.00 par value St. Josephs Hospital, Hartford, Wis. Second mortgage bonds Nos. 21-22-23-24 of the par value of $500.00 each.

$2000.00 par value St. Josephs Hospital, Hartford, Wis. Second mortgage bonds Nos. 25-26-27-28 of the par value of $500.00 each.

24     $500.00 par value Tegtmeyer Realty Company, Milwaukee, Wis. 1st mortgage leasehold bond No. 280.

$4500.00 par value Tegtmeyer Realty Company, Milwaukee, Wis. 1st mortgage leasehold bonds Nos. 317-347-348-349-350-360-364-400-401 of the par value of $500.00 each.

Endorsed: "Filed Oct. 22, 1931, Milton J. Knoblock, Referee."

25   ANSWER AND CROSS-PETITION OF KALT-ZIMMERS MANUFACTURING CO. to the petition of the West Side Bank, filed as follows:

* * (Caption) * *

And now comes Kalt-Zimmers Manufacturing Company, of the city of Milwaukee, State of Wisconsin, and, in answer to the petition of the West Side Bank filed in this matter and dated October 1, 1931, admits, denies, and alleges, as follows:

1. Admits that the West Side Bank is a banking corporation organized and existing under and by virtue of the laws of the State of Wisconsin, and located in the City of Milwaukee in the said state.

2. Admits that Hackett, Hoff & Thiermann, Inc. was duly adjudicated a bankrupt on the 8th day of June, 1931.

3. It denies knowledge or information sufficient to form a belief as to whether or not Hackett, Hoff & Thierman, Inc. was indebted to the said West Side Bank on said date, as set forth in the petition herein referred to, and thereunto puts the petitioner to its proof.

4. Admits that said Hackett, Hoff & Thiermann, Inc. attempted to pledge with said bank certain security as collateral to its indebtedness to said West Side Bank, but denies knowledge or information sufficient to form a belief as to what collateral was attempted to be pledged and to secure what debts the same were pledged, and thereunto puts the petitioner to its proof.

26   5. This answering respondent, in further answer to the said petition of the said West Side Bank herein referred to, and by way of cross-petition thereto, alleges:

(a)   That it is a corporation duly organized and existing under and by virtue of the laws of the State of Wisconsin, located at Milwaukee, Wisconsin.

(b)   That on or about the 15th day of August, A. D. 1929, it made, executed, and delivered to Hackett, Hoff & Thiermann, Inc., a corporation of the State of Wisconsin, as trustee, a certain mortgage or deed of trust wherein and whereby it conveyed to said Hackett, Hoff & Thiermann, Inc., as trustee, certain of its property located in the City of Milwaukee, as security for its Six Per Cent, Refunding First Mortgage Serial Gold Bonds of a total principal sum of One Hundred Fifteen Thousand Dollars ($115,000.00); that all of said bonds were duly executed by this answering respondent and duly certified by Hackett, Hoff & Thiermann, Inc., as trustee, as provided for in said deed of trust.

That said bonds issued pursuant to the terms of said trust mortgage contain, among other things, the following provision:

"Said bonds are issued under and secured by a mortgage or deed of trust of even date herewith, duly made, acknowledged and delivered by said Kalt-Zimmers Manufacturing Company to Hackett, Hoff & Thiermann, Incorporated, Trustee, to which deed of trust reference is hereby made with the same effect as though recited at length herein, for the description of the property mortgaged, the nature and extent of the security, the rights of the holders of the bonds, 27   and the terms and conditions upon which the said bonds are issued, held and secured, and may, before their fixed maturities, be declared at once due and payable, and the manner of prepayment before maturity."

(c)   This answering respondent further shows to the court that the said trust deed referred to in said bonds contains the following provisions:

"Whereas, there is an encumbrance existing against the premises above described, evidenced by a mortgage or deed of trust in the principal sum of Fifty-five Thousand Dollars ($55,000.00), dated the first day of January, 1923, recorded in the office of the Register of Deeds of Milwaukee County, Wisconsin, on the second day of January, 1923, in Volume 1087 of Mortgages, page 36, Document No. 1184879, and on which trust deed or mortgage there is unpaid a balance of principal of Thirty-five Thousand Dollars ($35,000.00);

"Now, Therefore, It Is Agreed, that said Trustee first set aside and hold a sufficient number of bonds or the proceeds of a sufficient number of bonds to fully pay and satisfy, as

soon as it can be done, the above mortgage in the principal sum of Fifty-five Thousand Dollars ($55,000.00); and after so setting aside such sufficient number of bonds or the proceeds of a sufficient number of bonds for the above purpose of paying and satisfying the above mortgage, the proceeds of the balance and remainder of said bonds shall then be paid out in liquidation of the cost of the contemplated build-
28   ing in course of erection or to be erected on said premises, upon architect's certificates issued from time to time for completed construction to date of such architect's certificates, and if any balance remains after the completion and full payment of said building, the balance is then to be at the disposal of the party of the first part.''

This answering respondent further shows that said mortgage of Fifty-five Thousand Dollars ($55,000.00), referred to in said trust deed, and the bonds secured thereby, were never paid and said mortgage was never satisfied.

(d)   This answering respondent further shows that none of the said Six Per Cent. Refunding First Mortgage bonds was ever sold by or for this respondent, that respondent never received any consideration therefor, and that the said Hackett, Hoff & Thiermann, Inc., gained possession thereof only as trustee under the said deed of trust, and that Eight Thousand Five Hundred Dollars ($8,500.00) par value of the said Six Per Cent. Refunding First Mortgage bonds secured by said trust indenture dated August 15, 1929, and issued by this answering respondent, are now in the possession of the petitioner, West Side Bank, under claim of title thereto as set forth in its petition herein referred to, and alleges that said West Side Bank has no right, title or interest in and to the said Eight Thousand Five Hundred Dollars ($8,500.00) par value of bonds issued by this answering respondent as herein set forth.

(e)   This answering respondent further alleges that M. H. Grossman has been and now is the duly elected, qualified and acting Trustee in Bankruptcy of Hackett, Hoff & Thiermann, Inc.

Wherefore, this answering respondent prays that the bonds issued by it dated on or about August 15, 1929, of the
29   aggregate principal amount of Eight Thousand Five Hundred Dollars ($8,500.00) and now held by the petitioner, West Side Bank, be ordered to be delivered to it by said West Side Bank, or that said bonds be delivered to M. H. Grossman, as trustee in bankruptcy for said Hackett, Hoff

& Thiermann, Inc., for the benefit and to the use of this answering respondent.

KALT-ZIMMERS MANUFACTURING COMPANY

By JOHN B. CASPER

Secretary.

FISH, MARSHUTZ & HOFFMAN,
  *Attorneys for Kalt-Zimmers Manu-
    facturing Company.*

30   United States of America,⎤
     State of Wisconsin,   ⎬ ss.
     Milwaukee County.   ⎦

JOHN B. CASPER, being first duly sworn, on oath deposes and says that he is the Secretary of the above and foregoing corporation, Kalt-Zimmers Manufacturing Company; that he has read the above and foregoing answer and cross-petition, and that the same is true of his own knowledge, except as to such matters therein stated on information and belief, and as to them he believes it to be true; that he makes this verification for and on behalf of said corporation and is authorized so to do.

JOHN B. CASPER

Subscribed and sworn to before me this 28th day of October, A. D. 1931.

FRANKLYN J. HARTMANN
*Notary Public, Milwaukee County,
Wisconsin.*

(N. S.)

My Commission expires: Sept. 16, 1934.

Endorsed: "Filed October 29, 1931 Milton J. Knoblock, Referee."

31   **ANSWER OF WEST SIDE BANK** to cross-petition of the Kalt-Zimmers Mfg. Co., filed as follows:

*   *   (Caption)   *   *

Now comes the petitioner, West Side Bank, of Milwaukee, and answering the cross-petition filed herein by said Kalt-Zimmers Mfg. Company, admits, denies, and alleges as follows:

1. Admits the allegations of paragraphs 5 (a) and 5 (b) of said cross-petition. That this petitioner attaches hereto a photostatic copy of one of said bonds, the others of said bonds

being of like form and tenor except as to number and amount, such photostatic copy hereto attached having been marked "Exhibit A" and is hereby made a part hereof as if fully set forth herein.

2. Admits that the trust deed referred to in paragraph 5 (c) of said cross-petition contains among other things the provisions alleged in said paragraph.

3. Denies any knowledge or information sufficient to form a belief as to the allegations set forth in paragraph 5 (c) of said cross-petition that the mortgage therein mentioned in the principal sum of Fifty-five Thousand Dollars ($55,000.00) and the bonds secured thereby were never paid and that said mortgage was never satisfied and petitioner demands strict proof thereof.

4. Denies any knowledge or information sufficient to form a belief as to the allegations set forth in paragraph 5 (d) of said cross-petition that none of said bonds therein mentioned were ever sold by or for said cross-petitioner and that said cross-petitioner never received any consideration therefor and said petitioner demands strict proof thereof.

32   5. Denies that said Hackett, Hoff & Thiermann, Inc. gained possession of said bonds only as trustee under the deed of trust mentioned in said cross-petition.

6. Admits that Eight Thousand Five Hundred Dollars ($8500.00) par value of said 5½% Refunding First Mortgage Serial Gold Bonds secured by the deed of trust dated August 15, 1929, mentioned in said cross-petition and issued by said Kalt-Zimmers Mfg. Company are now in the possession of this petitioner as set forth in its petition herein.

7. Denies that this petitioner has no right, title, or interest in or to said Eight Thousand Five Hundred Dollars ($8500.00) par value of said bonds issued by said Kalt-Zimmers Mfg. Company hereinbefore mentioned. Alleges that said bonds are negotiable instruments; that said petitioner became the holder thereof before maturity in good faith and for value; that said bonds were then complete and regular upon their face; that at the time the same were negotiated to this petitioner and it became the holder thereof, it had no notice of any infirmity in said bonds or defect in the title of said Hackett, Hoff & Thiermann, Inc., and that said petitioner took and received said bonds in the usual course of business; that said petitioner is the bona fide holder for value of said bonds.

8. Said petitioner further alleges that said Kalt-Zimmers Mfg. Company, delivered said bonds to said Hackett, Hoff &

Thiermann, Inc. and clothed said Hackett, Hoff & Thiermann, Inc. with apparent authority to transfer and negotiate the same, and that said Hackett, Hoff & Thiermann, Inc. did, within the apparent scope of its authority, transfer said bonds to this petitioner for a valuable consideration without notice of any limitation of its authority.

9.   Admits the allegations of paragraph 5 (e) of said cross-petition.

Wherefore, this petitioner prays that said cross-petition be dismissed with costs.

33

WEST SIDE BANK
By CHARLES KUHNMUENCH
President.

GEORGE A. AFFELDT
Attorney for West Side Bank.

State of Wisconsin } ss.
Milwaukee County

CHARLES KUHNMUENCH, being first duly sworn, on oath deposes and says that he is the President of the West Side Bank, the above named petitioner; that he makes this verification on its behalf and is duly authorized so to do; that he has read the foregoing answer to the cross-petition of Kalt-Zimmers Mfg. Company and knows the contents thereof, and that the same is true to his own knowledge except as to matters therein stated on information and belief, and as to such matters he believes it to be true; that the reason this verification is not made by said petitioner is that said petitioner is a corporation and deponent is such officer thereof and is acquainted with the facts; that the source of his information and the ground of his belief are the records and files of said corporation and statements made to him by officers and agents of said petitioner corporation in the regular course of their duty.

CHARLES KUHNMUENCH

Subscribed and sworn to before me this 3rd day of November, 1931.

GEORGE A. AFFELDT
*Notary Public, Milwaukee County,
Wisconsin.*

My Commission expires: Oct. 8, 1933.

Endorsed: "Received & Filed Nov. 4, 1931.   Milton J. Knoblock, Referee."

59   *   *   (Caption)   *   *

STATEMENT OF EVIDENCE.

Be it remembered that the above entitled matter came on regularly for hearing before Honorable Milton J. Knoblock, Referee in Bankruptcy, on the 17th day of October, 1932, and on adjourned dates, upon the issue formed by the petitions of the Marine National Exchange Bank of Milwaukee and West Side Bank and the cross petitions of Kalt-Zimmers Manufacturing Company and the answers thereto, Walter H. Bender, Esq., and Messrs. Bender, Trump, McIntyre & Freeman appearing as counsel for M. H. Grossman, Esq., Trustee in Bankruptcy, I. A. Fish, Esq., J. H. Marshutz, Esq., and Messrs. Fish, Marshutz & Hoffman appearing for Kalt-Zimmers Manufacturing Company, Leon E. Kaumheimer, Esq., Messrs. Kaumheimer & Kaumheimer and Douglass Van Dyke, Esq., appearing for the Marine National Exchange Bank of Milwaukee and George A. Affeldt, Esq., appearing for the West Side Bank.

It was then stipulated that the record taken in said matter should be applicable to the issue raised relating to the bonds held by the West Side Bank and to the issue raised relating to the bonds held by the Marine National Exchange Bank of Milwaukee, and that the two matters be heard and determined together.

CASE OF MARINE NATIONAL EXCHANGE BANK OF MILWAUKEE.

JOSEPH L. KENNEDY was then called as a witness by
60   the Marine National Exchange Bank of Milwaukee and testified as follows:

Direct Examination.

"I am the Assistant Cashier of the Marine National Exchange Bank of Milwaukee and have charge of the collateral records of the bank. I produce copies of the notes of Hackett, Hoff & Thiermann, Inc., held by the Marine National Exchange Bank of Milwaukee."

The copies of the notes were marked "BANK'S EXHIBITS A1, A2, A3, A4, A5 and A6". It was then stipulated that the copies of said exhibits may be produced and used with the same force and effect as if the or_igial notes had been pro-

duced. Said exhibits were then received in evidence. EX-HIBIT A5 is in the words and figures as follows, to-wit:
Milwaukee, Wisconsin, Feb. 2, 1931 $10,000.00

Thirty days after date we promise to pay to the order of Marine National Exchange Bank of Milwaukee, at its office Ten Thousand Dollars, for value received with interest at the rate of 6 percent. per annum, after maturity.

To secure the payment of this note and of any and all other liabilities of the undersigned to the holder hereof, howsoever created, arising or evidenced, or acquired by said holder, whether now or hereafter existing, and whether accrued or to become accrued, the undersigned has pledged, transferred and delivered to said Bank the following property, viz:

Various securities

The value of which is stated to be now _____ with the right to call for additional security should the value in the judgment of the holder decline; and on failure to supply the amount demanded, this obligation shall be deemed to be due and payable on demand, with full power and authority to sell and assign and deliver the whole of said property, or any part thereof, or any substitute therefor, or any additions thereto, at any Broker's Board, or at public or private sale, at the option of said holder, and with the right to be purchasers themselves at such Broker's Board, or public sale, on the non-performance of this promise, or the non-payment of any of the liabilities above mentioned, or at any time or times thereafter, without advertisement or notice. And after deducting all legal or other costs and expenses for collection, sale and delivery, to apply the residue of the proceeds of such sale or sales so to be made, to pay any, either or all of said liabilities when due, as said holder shall deem proper, return-ing the overplus to the undersigned, and in case of de-

61 ficiency the undersigned agree to pay the amount thereof forthwith after such sale. In case of the insolvency of the undersigned, any indebtedness due from the legal holder hereof to the undersigned may be appropriated and applied hereon. The holder of this note is hereby released from all duty or diligence in selling, enforcing, collecting or protest-ing any and all collaterals held with this note.

HACKETT, HOFF & THIERMANN, INC.
By (Signed) MAX L. THIERMANN,
Pres.
M. A. CHYBOWSKI,
Sec.

201 E. Michigan St.

Exhibits A1 to A6, inclusive, are identical in form and vary only in date, maturity and amount; each of said exhibits being promissory notes of Hackett, Hoff & Thiermann, Inc., payable to the order of the Marine National Exchange Bank of Milwaukee. The total principal due according to Exhibit A1 to Exhibit A6, inclusive, is $87,767.62.

"The notes produced were outstanding and unpaid on June 8, 1931, the date of the adjudication of Hacket, Hoff & Thiermann, Inc., as a bankrupt, except that the unpaid balance on Exhibit A6 was $2,767.62. I produce a statement of the debits and credits of the Hackett, Hoff & Thiermann, Inc., account made from the books of the Marine National Exchange Bank of Milwaukee covering the period from August 1, 1930, to October 22, 1931, which said statement shows the unpaid balance due from Hackett, Hoff & Thiermann, Inc."

Said statement was marked "EXHIBIT B" and was received in evidence. Said exhibit is in the words and figures, as follows:

	Date	Debit	Credit	Balance
	Aug. 1, 1930,			110,000.00
	Sep. 20, 1930,	15,000.00		125,000.00
	Dec. 22, 1930,	10,000.00		135,000.00
	Jan. 30, 1931,	40,000.00		175,000.00
62	Feb. 9, 1931,	15,000.00		190,000.00
	Feb. 21, 1931,		90,000.00	100,000.00
	Apr. 1, 1931,		10,000.00	90,000.00
	Apr. 3, 1931,		500.00	89,500.00
	Apr. 18, 1931,		1,000.00	88,500.00
	May 25, 1931,		732.38	87,767.62

			Dated	Due	Amount
Bk.	Ex.	A1	Mar. 14, 1929	Demand	$10,000.00
"	"	A2	Dec. 21, 1929	"	10,000.00
"	"	A3	Sep. 20, 1930	"	15,000.00
"	"	A4	Jan. 30, 1931	Mar. 2, 1931,	40,000.00
"	"	A5	Feb. 2, 1931	" 4, 1931,	10,000.00
"	"	A6	Feb. 9, 1931	" 11, 1931,	
				$15,000—Balance	3,500.00

$88,500.00

Balance of account of Hackett, Hoff & Thiermann, Inc., applied on note of Feb. 9th, 1931,   732.38

$87,767.62

"The statement shows only the loan account of Hackett, Hoff & Thiermann, Inc., and not the checking account, except that the balance in the checking account on May 25, 1931, amounting to $732.38, was applied on Exhibit A6."

"The loans of Hackett, Hoff & Thiermann, Inc., were secured by collateral, and on June 8, 1931, the bonds of Kalt-Zimmers Manufacturing Company were included in said collateral." The witness then produced the bonds, and they were received in evidence and marked as follows:
63　"BANK'S EXHIBIT C1 to BANK'S EXHIBIT C12, inclusive".

The exhibits are the bonds of Kalt-Zimmers Manufacturing Company and are identical in form, with the exception of the numbers and dates of maturity, a list of said bonds being as follows:

Exhibit C1 is Bond No.　99, Principal $500
"　　C2　"　　"　　"　100,　　"　　"
"　　C3　"　　"　　"　113,　　"　　"
"　　C4　"　　"　　"　116,　　"　　"
"　　C5　"　　"　　"　119,　　"　　"
"　　C6　"　　"　　"　120,　　"　　"
"　　C7　"　　"　　"　121,　　"　　"
"　　C8　"　　"　　"　122,　　"　　"
"　　C9　"　　"　　"　123,　　"　　"
"　　C10　"　　"　　"　124,　　"　　"
"　　C11　"　　"　　"　125,　　"　　"
"　　C12　"　　"　　"　138,　　"　　"

The form of said bonds appears from the photostat attached to the answer of the Marine National Exchange Bank of Milwaukee to the cross petition of the Kalt-Zimmers Manufacturing Company and from "West Side Exhibit C6" attached hereto.

"I have prepared a summary of the transaction of the Marine National Exchange Bank of Milwaukee with Hackett, Hoff & Thiermann, Inc., with respect to the bonds of the Kalt-Zimmers Manufacturing Company now on hand. The statement shows the number of the bonds, the par value, the date received and the nature of the transaction giving rise to the collateral or the security exchanged for said bonds."

The statement was marked "Bank's Exhibit D". It was then stipulated that the books of the Marine National Exchange Bank of Milwaukee would show what is shown on Exhibit D and that the books of the Marine National Exchange

Bank of Milwaukee need not be produced for that purpose. EXHIBIT D was then received in evidence.

"The statement shows that bond No. 99 of the Kalt-Zimmers Manufacturing Company was exchanged in the ordinary course of business for bond No. 158 of Manufacturers' Sites Corporation. Bond No. 100 of the Kalt-Zimmers Manu-
64   facturing Company was exchanged in the usual course of business for bond No. 57 of Tegtmeyer Realty Company. Likewise, bonds No. 113, 116 and 138 were exchanged for other bonds of the same face amount that were held as collateral. Bonds No. 119 to 125 were received by the Marine National Exchange Bank of Milwaukee on January 30, 1931, as part of the collateral for a loan of $40,000 made to Hackett, Hoff & Thiermann, Inc. The bonds surrendered at the time of the exchange for the Kalt-Zimmers Manufacturing Company bonds were equal in value as collateral to the value of the bonds of the Kalt-Zimmers Manufacturing Company."

Cross-Examination.

"In addition to the loan account of Hackett, Hoff & Thiermann, Inc., at the Marine National Exchange Bank, Hackett, Hoff & Thiermann had a checking account. The proceeds of the loans to Hackett, Hoff & Thiermann, Inc., were placed in the checking account. The collateral for the loans is miscellaneous bonds. The list of the collateral is attached to the petition of the Marine National Exchange Bank of Milwaukee relating to the sale of said collateral. The bonds of Kalt-Zimmers Manufacturing Company are still held as collateral to the loans."

CASE OF WEST SIDE BANK.

CHARLES KUHNMUENCH was called as a witness by the West Side Bank and testified as follows:

Direct Examination.

"I am the President of the West Side Bank and was such officer during 1929, 1930, and 1931. During that time, the West Side Bank made loans on collateral security to Hackett, Hoff & Thiermann, Inc. At the time of the adjudication of Hackett, Hoff & Thiermann, Inc., as a bankrupt, it was indebted to the West Side Bank on five notes aggregating a principal amount of $71,515.47.''

65   WEST SIDE EXHIBIT A1 is in the words and figures as follows, to-wit:

$10,000.00   Milwauke, Wis., March 6th, 1931

Sixty days after date we promise to pay to the order of West Side Bank, of Milwaukee, Wis.,

Ten Thousand .... Dollars, for value received, with interest at the rate of 6½ per cent per annum, after date having deposited with said Bank as collateral security, for payment of this or any other liability or liabilities of .... to said Bank, due or to become due, or that may be hereafter contracted or existing, howsoever acquired by said Bank, the following property, viz:

Various securities

The market value of which is now $............; with the right to call for additional security should the same decline; and on failure to respond, this obligation shall be deemed to be due and payable on demand, with full power and authority to sell and assign and deliver the whole of said property, or any part thereof, or any substitute therefor, or any additions thereto, at any Brokers' Board, or at public or private sale, at the option of said Bank or its assigns, and with the right to be purchasers themselves at such Brokers' Board, or public sale, on the non-performance of this promise, or the non-payment of any of the liabilities above mentioned, or at any time or times thereafter, without advertisement or notice. And after deducting all legal or other costs and expenses for collection, sale and delivery, to apply the reisdue of the proceeds of such sale or sales so to be made, to pay any, either or all of said liabilities, as said Bank or its President or Cashier shall deem proper, returning the overplus to the undersigned. In case of the insolvency of the undersigned, any indebtedness due from the legal holder hereof to the undersigned may be appropriated and applied hereon at any time, as well before as after the maturity hereof.

HACKETT, HOFF & THIERMANN, INC.
W. F. KEMBE,
Vice P.
M. A. CHYBOWSKI,
Sec.

West Side Exhibits A1 to A5, inclusive, are identcal in form
and vary only in date, maturity date and amount, Exhibit A2
being note, dated April 8, 1931, due May 8, 1931, for the
66   sum of $20,000.00, Exhibit A3 being note, dated April 28,
1931, due May 28, 1931, for $5,000.00, Exhibit A4 being
note, dated March 31, 1931, due May 30, 1931, for $10,000.00,
and Exhibit A5 being note, dated April 4, 1931, due June 3,
1931, for $27,500.00.

"Hackett, Hoff & Thiermann, Inc., also carried a checking
account at the West Side Bank. I produce the ledger sheets
of the West Side Bank showing the loan transactions with
Hackett, Hoff & Thiermann, Inc." The ledger sheets were
marked "WEST SIDE EXHIBIT B1, WEST SIDE EX-
HIMIT B2 and WEST SIDE EXHIBIT B3" and were received in evidence.

"Exhibits No. B1, B2 and B3 of the West Side Bank show
the debits and credits in connection with the loan account of
Hackett, Hoff & Thiermann, Inc., and the balance on June 8,
1931, was $71,515.47. The loans were secured by deposit of
bonds, and from time to time some of the bonds were withdrawn and others substituted in their place. The loan is now
secured by bonds deposited as collateral. On June 8, 1931,
the date of the adjudication of Hackett, Hoff & Thiermann,
Inc., as a bankrupt, the West Side Bank held the bonds of the
Kalt-Zimmers Manufacturing Company, which I now produce, as collateral security for the payment of these notes."

The bonds were marked "WEST SIDE EXHIBITS C1 to
C12, both inclusive" and were received in evidence. The
bonds are all bonds of the Kalt-Zimmers Manufacturing Company, identical in form and substance, with the exception of
numbers, maturities and amounts, said bonds being as follows:

Exhibit C1, bond number 62, principal $1,000
"   C2,   "   "   66,   "   1,000
"   C3,   "   "   72,   "   1,000
"   C4,   "   "   73,   "   1,000
"   C5,   "   "   74,   "   1,000
"   C6,   "   "   94,   "   500
"   C7,   "   "   95,   "   500
"   C8,   "   "   96,   "   500
"   C9,   "   "   110,   "   500
"   C10,   "   "   128,   "   500
"   C11,   "   "   129,   "   500
"   C12,   "   "   130,   "   500

Permission was granted to withdraw said exhibits and
67   to substitute therefor a photostatic copy of Exhibit C6,
being bond number 94. A photostatic copy of said exhibit is hereto attached.

"The West Side Bank received Exhibit C1, bond No. 62
and bond No. 66 on October 9, 1930 and bonds Nos. 72, 72 and
74 on October 3, 1930. On October 3, 1930, the West Side
Bank surrendered to Hackett, Hoff & Thiermann, in exchange
for bonds of Kalt-Zimmers Manufacturing Company, bonds
of the Milwaukee Novelty Dye Works. At the time of the surrender of the Milwaukee Novelty Dye Works bonds, said
bonds were then in good standing. The bonds received on
October 9, 1930, were received as collateral for a loan. Exhibit C6, bond No. 94, Exhibit C7, bond No. 95, and Exhibit
C8, bond No. 96, were received on July 28, 1930. On that
date, the West Side Bank delivered to Hackett, Hoff & Thiermann, Inc., two bonds of Kalt-Zimmers Manufacturing Company and five North Shore Building Bonds, and received the
bonds of the Kalt-Zimmers Manufacturing Company and
other bonds in lieu thereof. On the date mentioned, the bonds
surrendered were in good standing. Exhibit C9, bond No. 110
was received from Hackett, Hoff & Thiermann, Inc., on November 14, 1929, and on that date an additional loan was
made, said loan amounting to $5,000, and the bond of the Kalt-
Zimmers Manufacturing Company was one of the bonds received as collateral. Exhibits C10, C11 and C12, being bonds
Nos. 128, 129 and 130 were received by the West Side Bank
on October 14, 1929. On that date, there was surrendered to
Hackett, Hoff & Thiermann, Inc., bonds aggregating $5,000 in
amount that were in good standing and, among others, the
bonds of the Kalt-Zimmers Manufacturing Company were
substituted as collateral. Each of the bonds was received by
the West Side Bank in the regular course of business and
have been held by the West Side Bank since the date they
were received from Hackett, Hoff & Thiermann, Inc."

Cross-Examination.

"The West Side Bank received bonds number 72 and 73
on April 25, 1930, and surrendered them to Hackett, Hoff
68   & Thiermann, Inc., on July 28, 1930. The bonds when
received were collateral for the loan account of Hackett,
Hoff & Thiermann, Inc. Hackett, Hoff & Thiermann, Inc., also
had a checking account at the bank and in case of a new loan,

the money was deposited in said checking account. West Side Exhibit D is the ledger sheet of the checking account of Hackett, Hoff & Thiermann, Inc., and it shows credits to the account. The balance of the checking account was applied by the West Side Bank on the loan account on May 5, 1931, said balance amounting to $1,092.86.''

CASE OF KALT-ZIMMERS MANUFACTURING COMPANY.

Kalt-Zimmers Manufacturing Company by its attorney produced a certain trust deed which was marked ''KALT-ZIMMERS EXHIBIT 1'' and was received in evidence, said exhibit being a trust deed of Kalt-Zimmers Manufacturing Company to Hackett, Hoff & Thiermann, Inc., trustee, dated August 15, 1929, and recorded in the office of the Register of Deeds on October 12, 1929. Said exhibit is in the words and figures as follows, except as to the parts of which an abridgement is set forth and noted, to-wit:

''This Indenture, made as of the fifteenth day of August, A. D. 1929, by and between Kalt-Zimmers Manufacturing Company, a corporation organized and existing under and by virtue of the laws of the State of Wisconsin, located at Milwaukee, Wisconsin, party of the first part and hereinafter called ''first party'', and Hackett, Hoff & Thiermann, Incorporated, a corporation duly organized and existing under and by virtue of the laws of the State of Wisconsin, having its office at No. 77 East Michigan Street, Milwaukee, Wisconsin, as Trustee, and hereinafter called ''Trustee'', party of the second part;

Witnesseth: That Whereas, said first party, in the exercise of its powers and in order to obtain money and for other lawful purposes of its corporation, and in accordance with resolutions duly adopted by a majority of its board of directors and by the holders of a majority of its stock, at meetings of its board of directors and stockholders, all of which meetings 69 were duly called and held for that purpose, and with the consent of holders of a majority of its stock, and for the purpose of securing certain bonds, hereinafter more fully described, which said bonds are in form, with the exception of the numbers, denominations and dates of maturity, substantially as follows:''

(For form of bond, interest coupon and Trustee's certificate, see Marine Bank's Exhibit A attached to answer to cross petition and West Side's Exhibit C6.)

(Abridged)   The Kalt-Zimmers Manufacturing Company "in order to secure equally the payment of interest and principal of the bonds aforesaid at any time outstanding, whether issued contemporaneously with the execution of this mortgage, or hereafter duly issued under the terms hereof" conveys certain real estate to Hackett, Hoff & Thiermann, Inc., as Trustee.

"To Have and To Hold the premises, real and personal property, rights, privileges, estate and appurtenances hereby conveyed and assigned, or intended to be conveyed and assigned, unto the said Trustee, its successors and assigns, forever.

In Trust, Nevertheless, for the equal and pro rate benefit and security of all and every holder of the bonds and interest coupons issued under and secured by this Indenture, or such as shall at any time become or be from time to time the purchaser or holder of the bonds hereinbefore described and hereby secured, and for the purposes hereinafter expressed, to-wit:

(1)   It is hereby understood and agreed that said issue of One Hundred Fifteen Thousand Dollars ($115,000.00) of bonds, hereby provided for, shall, upon the signing and execution hereof, or as soon after as practicable, be duly certified by the Trustee and negotiated and sold by the Trustee; and said Trustee shall first set aside sufficient bonds or the proceeds of sufficient bonds to pay off that certain trust deed or mortgage in the principal sum of Fifty-five Thousand Dollars ($55,000.00), hereinafter described; the balance of said 70   proceeds of said bonds, so sold, shall then be disbursed by said Trustee as hereinafter provided."

(Abridged)   (2)   The Trustee is to receive from the first party the sums of money covenanted to be paid to it and upon satisfaction of the terms of the mortgage to execute a release of the same.

(Abridged)   (3)   The Trustee shall receive from the first party all insurance policies and statements, and may demand the production of the same.

(Abridged)   (4)   In case of default by the first party as to any condition of the mortgage, the Trustee shall have the right for the holders of the bonds to foreclose said mortgage, except that the holders of the bonds shall have the right to require the Trustee to declare the mortgage due and to foreclose the same.

(Abridged)   (5)   The Trustee shall, upon payment of the

bonds and coupons, cancel the same and return them to the first party and upon complete payment, release the mortgage.

(Abridged) The party of the first part covenants in the usual form that it is seized of a good and perfect title to the premises conveyed.

(Abridged) The party of the first part agrees that the interest in the real estate arising by reason of the mortgage shall be taxed with the interest of the first party in said real estate.

"Whereas, there is an encumbrance existing against the premises above described, evidenced by a mortgage or deed of trust in the principal sum of Fifty-five Thousand Dollars ($55,000.00), dated the first day of January, 1923, recorded in the office of the Register of Deeds of Milwaukee County, Wisconsin, on the second day of January, 1923, in Volume 1087 of Mortgages, page 36, Document No. 1184879, and on which trust deed or mortgage there is unpaid a balance of principal of Thirty-five Thousand Dollars ($35,000.00);

71   Now, Therefore, It Is Agreed, that said Trustee first set aside and hold a sufficient number of bonds or the proceeds of a sufficient number of bonds to fully pay and satisfy, as soon as it can be done, the above mortgage in the principal sum of Fifty-five Thousand Dollars ($55,000.00); and after so setting aside such sufficient number of bonds or the proceeds of a sufficient number of bonds for the above purpose of paying and satisfying the above mortgage, the proceeds of the balance and remainder of said bonds shall then be paid out in liquidation of the cost of the contemplated building in course of erection or to be erected on said premises, upon architect's certificates issued from time to time for completed construction to date of such architect's certificates, and if any balance remains after the completion and full payment of said building, the balance is then to be at the disposal of the party of the first part."

(Abridged) It is covenanted that if the party of the first part pay the sum of $115,000.00 with interest according to the terms of 200 bonds, the mortgage shall be null and void.

(Abridged) The party of the first part agrees to pay the principal and interest due on each of the bonds when the same is due, and to pay all taxes levied or assessed against the property conveyed. It is further provided that upon non-payment of any amount due, the whole amount unpaid might be declared forthwith due and payable, and an action commenced to foreclose the mortgage upon certain terms therein stated.

(Abridged) It is provided that within certain limitations, the Trustee shall receive the proceeds of insurance money arising out reason of damage to the mortgaged premises, and use the same for certain specified purposes.

(Abridged) "The said bonds secured by this trust deed or mortgage shall pass by delivery", except that they may be registered by the Trustee, and in such case shall pass only upon transfer upon the books of the Trustee.

(Abridged) In the event of default existing for the length of time required by the mortgage, the Trustee shall, upon the written request of twenty per cent. (20%) of the holders of the bonds, declare all amounts due.

72

(Abridged) The holders of more than eighty per cent. (80%) in amount of the bonds outstanding, may, by written direction, waive any default, except that all of the bondholders of bonds payable on a particular date must consent to extend the time for the payment of principal for a period beyond ninety (90) days.

(Abridged) The party of the first part shall have the right to accelerate payment in the sum of Five Thousand Dollars ($5,000) or more on unmatured bonds, by giving the notice and making the payments required by the terms of said paragraph.

(Abridged) Upon the maturity of the bonds, the party of the first part shall pay to the trustee the amount due thereon and the Trustee shall release said mortgage, and the first party shall not be responsible for the application of the amount paid to the Trustee.

(Abridged) The first party shall be entitled to the possession of the mortgaged premises as long as there is no default as to any of the provisions or conditions contained in the mortgage. The Trustee may advance sums of money required to repair defaults, and if it shall do so, it shall have a first lien upon the mortgaged premises for the amount so advanced.

(Abridged) The first party agrees to deposit with the Trustee all payments of principal and interest at least five (5) days before the same are due.

(Abridged) The Trustee may resign upon giving the required notice, and a successor Trustee may be appointed.

(Abridged) Action taken by the Trustee with the consent of any person being the holder of a bond shall be conclusive upon future holders of said bonds.

(Abridged) In case of foreclosure, upon the request of

seventy-five per cent. (75%) or more of the outstanding
73   bonds, the Trustee may bid and become the purchaser at
the foreclosure sale.

(Abridged)   In the event of the loss or mutilation of a
bond, the Trustee may issue a new bond upon satisfactory
proof and indemnity and make a reasonable charge therefor.

"The Trustee hereby accepts and assumes the duties herein imposed and agrees to authenticate the bonds in accordance with the following additional terms:"

(Abridged)   (1) The recitals of fact contained in the bond
are not construed to be made by the Trustee.

(Abridged)   (2) The Trustee makes no representation as
to the validity of the indenture or the value of any bond or
coupon.

(Abridged)   (3) The Trustee shall not be liable for acting
in accordance with any notice or request of any person if it is
believed that said person is a bondholder.

(Abridged)   (4) The Trustee shall receive reasonable compensation for its services and have a first lien therefor.

(Abridged)   (5) The Trustee shall not be liable for neglect
or wrong doing if it has exercised reasonable care in the
selection of its agents and employees.

"(6)   The Trustee or any of its officers, agents or stockholders may acquire, own and deal in said bonds and coupons
with the same rights as if not Trustee hereunder and shall not
be obliged to account to anyone for any profits made thereby."

(Abridged)   (7) The Trustee shall not be required to take
any action or start any suit unless satisfactorily indemnified.

(Abridged)   (8) The Trustee shall not be held to have
notice of defaults or other facts unless it receives notice from
twenty per cent. (20%) or more of the bondholders.

(Signatures and acknowledgements omitted.)

74   MARK W. RAHN was then called as a witness by Kalt-
       Zimmers Manufacturing Company and testified as
       follows:

Direct Examination.

"I am a certified public accountant employed by Einbecker,
McCormack & Kegel, and I have examined the books of
Hackett, Hoff & Thiermann, Inc. The books were at the time
of the examination in the possession of the Trustee in Bankruptcy. I made a written report of my audit."

The audit was received in evidence, subject to the objection of the Marine National Exchange Bank of Milwaukee to
such legal conclusions as are therein contained, and marked
"KALT-ZIMMERS EXHIBIT 2."

"Exhibit 1 contained in Kalt-Zimmers Exhibit 2 shows the
amount of Kalt-Zimmers first refunding mortgage bonds
pledged on various dates by Hackett, Hoff & Thiermann, Inc.,
as collateral." The words and figures contained therein are
as follows:

Date	Total Bonds Used as Collateral
Oct. 14, 1929	$ 1,500.00
Nov. 14, 1929	500.00
Apr. 15, 1930	500.00
Apr. 27, 1930	1,000.00
July 28, 1930	1,500.00
Oct. 2, 1930	2,000.00
Oct. 9, 1930	2,000.00
Nov. 19, 1930	500.00
Dec. 1, 1930	4,000.00
Jan. 9, 1931	500.00
Jan. 19, 1931	1,000.00
Jan. 30, 1931	3,500.00
	$18,500.00

"Exhibit 2 of said Exhibit 2 shows the bonds so deposited
with the Marine National Exchange Bank and with the West
Side Bank." The words and figures contained therein are as
follows:

75

Date	Issue	Bond Number	Marine National Exchange Bank	West Side Bank
Oct. 9, 1930	1st Ref. Mortgage............	62	....	$1,000.00
Oct. 9, 1930	do	66	....	1,000.00
Apr. 27, 1930	do	72	....	1,000.00
Oct. 2, 1930	do	73	....	1,000.00
Oct. 2, 1930	do	74	....	1,000.00
Dec. 2, 1930		93	$ 500.00	....
July 28, 1930		94	....	500.00
July 28, 1930		95	....	500.00
July 28, 1930		96	....	500.00
Apr. 15, 1930		99	500.00	....
Jan. 9, 1931		100	500.00	....
Nov.14, 1929		110	....	500.00
Nov.19, 1930		113	500.00	....
Jan. 19, 1931		116	500.00	....
Jan. 30, 1931		119	500.00	....
Jan. 30, 1931		120	500.00	....
Jan. 30, 1931		121	500.00	....
Jan. 30, 1931		122	500.00	....
Jan. 30, 1931		123	500.00	....
Jan. 30, 1931		124	500.00	....
Jan. 30, 1931		125	500.00	....
Oct. 14, 1929		128	....	500.00
Oct. 14, 1929		129	....	500.00
Oct. 14, 1929		130	....	500.00
Jan. 19, 1931		138	500.00	....
Apr. 1, 1931		93	500.00	....
			$6,000.00	$8,500.00

"Exhibit 4 of said Exhibit 2 shows the history of sales and purchases of bond by Hackett, Hoff & Thiermann, Inc." The words and figures contained therein are as follows:

Date	Explanation	Dr.	Cr.	Balance
1929				
Sept. 6th	1st Ref. M'tge. bonds....	$115,000.00	$........	$........
Sept. 6th to				
Sept. 30th	Sales—various..........	....	800.00	....
Oct. 9th	Balance................	....	....	114,200.00
Oct. 9th to				
Oct. 12th	Sales—various..........	....	100.00	....
Oct. 14th	Balance................	....	....	114,100.00
Nov. 4th to				
Nov. 12th	Sales—various..........	....	19,700.00	....
Nov. 8th	Repurchases—various....	100.00	....	....
Nov. 14th	Balance................	....	....	94,500.00
Dec. 30th	Repurchases—various....	100.00	....	....
Nov. 27th to				
Jan. 8, 1930	Sales—various..........	....	38,500.00	....
1930				
Jan. 9th	Sales—58-59-60-61-62......	....	4,850.00	....
Jan. 9th	Balance................	....	....	51,250.00

76

Date	Explanation	Dr.	Cr.	Balance
1930				
Jan. 9th to				
Jan. 13th	Sales—various...........	$........	$ 5,000.00	$........
Jan. 13th	Balance due on bonds			
	58-59-60-61-62..........	....	150.00	....
Jan. 16th to				
Jan. 17th	Sales—various..........	....	2,000.00	....
Jan. 17th	Repurchases—various....	2,000.00	....	....
Jan. 20th to				
Jan. 22nd	Sales—various..........	....	899.27	....
Jan. 22nd to				
Jan. 29th	Repurchases—various....	3,900.00	....	....
Jan. 22nd to				
Jan. 30th	Sales—various..........	....	9,500.73	....
Jan. 27th	Repurchase—bonds 62-108	1,500.00	....	....
Jan. 30th	Sales—bond 113..........	....	500.00	....
Jan. 30th	Balance.................	....	....	40,600.00
Jan. 31st	Sales—bonds 70-71-72-73-74	....	5,000.00	....
Jan. 31st	Balance.................	....	....	35,600.00
Feb. 1st to				
Feb. 3rd	Sales—various..........	....	899.62	....
Feb. 4th	Repurchases—various....	2,000.00	....	....
Feb. 10th to				
Feb. 13th	Sales—various..........	....	.38	....
Feb. 13th	Sales—bond 116..........	....	500.00	....
Feb. 13th	Balance.................	....	....	36,200.00
Feb. 21st	Repurchases—various....	100.00	....	....
Feb. 21st to				
Mar. 6th	Sales—various..........	....	5,700.00	....
Mar. 19th	Repurchases—various....	100.00	....	....
Mar. 25th	Repurchase—bonds 70-71-			
	72-73-74...............	5,000.00	....	....
Mar. 28th	Repurchases—various....	100.00	....	....
Mar. 20th to				
Apr. 5th	Sales—various..........	....	2,095.00	....
Apr. 7th	Repurchases—various....	200.00	....	....
Apr. 7th to				
Apr. 10th	Sales—various..........	....	1,905.00	....
Apr. 15th	Balance.................	....	....	32,000.00
Apr. 27th	Balance.................	....	....	32,000.00
May 7th	Sales—various..........	....	2,000.00	....
May 12th	Repurchases—various....	100.00	....	....
May 15th	Sales—various..........	....	100.00	....
June 9th	Repurchases—various....	1,000.00	....	....
June 16th	Sales—various..........	....	1,000.00	....
June 30th	Repurchases—various....	200.00	....	....
July 8th to				
July 16th	Sales—various..........	....	700.00	....
July 28th	Sales—bonds 62-66-67-68-			
	69-70-71-72-73-74........	....	10,000.00	....
July 28th	Balance.................	....	....	19,500.00
Aug. 1st	Repurchases—various....	100.00	....	....
Aug. 26th	Repurchases—various....	1,500.00	....	....
Aug. 26th	Sales—various..........	....	1,100.00	....
Oct. 2nd	Repurchase—bonds 62-66-			
	67-68-69-70-71-72-73-74...	10,000.00	....	....
Oct. 2nd	Balance.................	....	....	30,000.00

77

Date	Explanation	Dr.	Cr.	Balance
1930				
Oct. 9th	Balance.................	$........	$........	$ 30,000.00
Oct. 2nd to				
Oct. 14th	Sales—various..........	....	5,000.00	....
Nov. 6th to				
Nov. 8th	Repurchases—various....	2,500.00	....	....
Nov. 7th	Sales—various..........	....	2,000.00	....
Nov.19th	Balance.................	....	....	25,500.00
Dec. 1st	Repurchase—116-178-179..	700.00	....	....
Dec. 1st	Balance.................	....	....	26,200.00
Dec. 1st to				
Dec. 15th	Sales—various..........	....	1,100.00	....
Dec. 1st to				
Jan. 6, 1931	Repurchases—various....	4,100.00	....	....
1931				
Jan. 6th to				
Jan. 7th	Sales—various..........	....	1,200.00	....
Jan. 9th	Balance.................	....	....	28,000.00
Jan. 9th to				
Jan. 19th	Repurchases—various....	1,100.00	....	....
Jan. 9th to				
Jan. 19th	Sales—various..........	....	2,000.00	....
Jan. 19th	Balance.................	....	....	27,100.00
Jan. 30th	Balance.................	....	....	27,100.00
Feb. 17th to				
Apr. 1st	Sales—various..........	....	2,200.00	....
Mar. 19th	Repurchases—various....	100.00	....	....
July 21st	Bonds—67-68-69-70 charged to account of Max L. Thiermann..........	....	4,000.00	....
	Final balance...........	....	....	21,000.00

Note.—Balances of January 9th-January 19th and January 30th, 1931, include bond number 129 of the first mortgage issue—cost $1,000.00.

"Exhibit 5 of said Exhibit 2 is an analysis of the account of Kalt-Zimmers Manufacturing Company showing payments made by Hackett, Hoff & Thiermann, Inc., on behalf of Kalt-Zimmers Manufacturing Company and the balance due to Kalt-Zimmers Manufacturing Company on the dates mentioned." The words and figures contained in said exhibit are as follows:

Date	Explanation	Source.	Dr.	Cr.	Balance due Kalt-Zimmers
1929					
Sept. 6th	1st Ref. Mtge. bonds (entry as of Oct. 31, 1929)............	....	$........	$115,000.00	$........
Sept. 26th	Abst. and Art. of Inc..	Ck.&JV	32.80	....	....
Sept. 28th	Bonds sold—Manitowoc Products Co.—Nos. 289-302-303-304-305 and interest........	JV	....	5,053.17	....

78

Date	Explanation	Source	Dr.	Cr.	Balance due Kalt-Zimmers
1929					
Sept. 27th	Bonds purchased— Allen-Bradley Co.— Nos. 582-583-584-585-586 and int.........	JV	$5,019.87	$	$ ....
Sept. 27	Check to balance bond sale and purchase...	Ck	33.10	....	....
Oct. 7th	10 copies Art. of Inc...	Ck	6.60	....	....
Oct. 9th	Balance..............	....	....	....	114,960.80
Oct. 14th	Expense on bonds, stamps and recording deed..............	Ck	65.76	....	....
Oct. 14th	Filing fees and appraisal	Ck	157.50	....	....
Oct. 14th	Balance..............	....	....	....	114,737.54
Oct. 18th	Appraisal survey and map..............	JV	115.00	....	....
Oct. 23rd	Printing bonds, forms and abstracts.......	JV	185.00	....	....
Nov. 1st	U. S. Treasury notes and interest.........	....	....	4,054.56	....
Nov. 1st	Allen-Bradley Co.— bonds — 582-583-584-585-586 and int......	JV	....	5,062.44	....
Nov. 1st	Fairmount Riding Academy—1/2 and interest.............	....	....	3,057.50	....
Nov. 1st	Treselro Realty Co.— Nos. 262-264-265-266 and int.............	....	....	2,018.00	....
Nov. 1st	H. Mason—Nos. 32-33-34-35 and int.......	....	....	4,060.00	....
Nov. 1st	St. Helen's—Nos. 36-37-38 and int.......	....	....	1,504.00	....
Nov. 1st	St. Alexander's—Nos. 26-27-28-29-32-33-34 and int.............	....	....	3,561.83	....
Nov. 2nd	Cash...............	Ck	13,180.31	....	....
Nov. 2nd	E. Brielmaier & Sons Co. certificate......	Ck	2,400.00	....	....
Nov. 11th	H. Schmitt & Son, Inc., certificate..........	....	6,000.00	....	....
Nov. 14th	do	....	3,071.16	....	....
Nov. 14th	Balance..............	....	....	....	113,104.40
Nov. 20th and Nov. 22nd	Payment on cert. of contractor..........	....	4,564.85	....	....
Nov. 26th	Check int. on bonds...	....	137.94	....	....
Nov. 27th	Engineer's fees........	....	25.00	....	....
Dec. 10 to Dec. 21st	Payments to contractors.............	....	26,735.00	....	....
Dec. 31st	Commission on loan...	JV	5,750.00	....	....
Dec. 31st	Legal service.........	....	500.00	....	....

78

Date	Explanation	Source	Dr.	Cr.	Balance due Kalt-Zimmers
1930					
Jan. 2nd	Tegtmeyer Realty Co. —bond and int......	......	....	1,015.00	....
Jan. 9th	Balance...............	....	....	....	76,406.61
Jan. 10th to Jan. 21st	Payments to con- tractors.............	......	26,402.54	....	....
Jan. 30th	Balance...............	......	....	......	50,004.07
Jan. 31st	do	......	....	....	50,004.07
Feb. 11th	Payments to con- tractors.............	......	6,533.80	....	....
Feb. 10th	To balance various bond transactions...	......	.28	....	....
Feb. 13th	Balance.	......	....	....	43,469.99
Feb. 20th to Apr. 10th	Payments to con- tractors.............	......	10,794.48	....	....
March 26th	Balance principal due first mtge...........	......	1,000.00	....	....
Mar. 26th	Int. on refunding issue.	......	726.38	....	....
Mar. 26th	Tax due on ref. issue...	......	69.00	....	....
Mar. 26th	Insurance account.....	......	310.77	....	....
Apr. 15th	Balance...............	......	......	....	30,569.36
Apr. 22nd	Window Guards.......	......	196.00	....	....
Apr. 27th	Balance	......	....	....	30,373.36
May 12th	Midwest Ventilating Works—extra work..	......	99.96	....	....
June 9th	Insurance account re- fund...	......	....	31.03	....
June 9th	Commission allowance 5% $30,000.00.......	......	....	1,500.00	....
July 22nd	Tax refund............	......	....	18.00	....
July 28th	Balance...............	......	....	....	31,822.43
Sept. 8th	Insurance account.....	......	77.89	....	....
Oct. 2nd	Balance.....	......	....	....	31,744.54
Oct. 9th	do	......	....	....	31,744.54
Oct. 22nd	Serial principal-refund- ing mortgage due August 15, 1930.....	......	5,000.00	....	....
Nov. 19th	Balance...............	......	....	....	26,744.54
Dec. 1st	do	......	....	....	26,744.54
Dec. 30th	Insurance	......	35.48	....	....
Dec. 30th	Cash................	......	....	4,246.99	....
Dec. 30th	Interest on first mort- gage balance........	......	975.00	....	....
Dec. 30th	Tax.................	......	19.50	....	....
Dec. 30th	Interest adjustment— Aug. 15th to Dec. 30th................	......	....	38.45	....
1931					
Jan. 9th	Balance...............	......	......	....	30,000.00
Jan. 19th	do	......	....	....	30,000.00
Jan. 30th	do	......	....	....	30,000.00
Feb. 28th	Serial principal—first mortgage due Jan. 1, 1931................	......	5,000.00	....	....
July 21st	Balance...............	......	....	....	25,000.00

"Exhibit 6 of said Exhibit 2 is a summary of the other exhibits showing the bonds used as collateral and the amount due Kalt-Zimmers Manufacturing Company on open account at the various dates. Exhibit 7 of the report shows the account of the first mortgage of Kalt-Zimmers Manufacturing Company detailing the retirement of said bonds and showing that the outstanding bonds on February 28, 1931 amounted to $25,000.00. This is the account of the first mortgage referred to in the trust deed hereinbefore received in evidence. Exhibit 8 of said Exhibit 2 is an analysis of the payments made on the first refunding mortgage and shows that payments totalling $5,000.00 have been made, leaving a balance of $110,-000.00 in bonds still outstanding as per the books of Hackett, Hoff & Thiermann, Inc. Exhibit 10 of said Exhibit 2 contains a record of the bonds in the possession of the Trustee in Bankruptcy, and it shows that bonds totalling $6,500.00 in amount are still held by said trustee. Exhibits 11 and 12 of said Exhibit 2 show the retirement dates for each of the bonds of the first mortgage and of the first refunding mortgage respectively."

Whereupon counsel for Kalt-Zimmers Manufacturing Company asked the witness whether Hackett, Hoff & Thiermann, Inc., had at any time paid to Kalt-Zimmers Manufacturing Company, or on its behalf, more money than had been received from the sale of bonds. Counsel for the Marine National Exchange Bank of Milwaukee and the West Side Bank objected to said question for the reason that it was incompetent, irrelevant and immaterial. Said objection was overruled, and an exception was then and there taken, and the witness answered that at no time had more money been paid than had been received from the sale of bonds.

Whereupon counsel for the Kalt-Zimmers Manufacturing Company asked the witness whether Hackett, Hoff & Thiermann, Incorporated at any time had in its possession more unpledged bonds than were required by the refunding mortgage to be held for the retirement of the first mortgage. Counsel for the Marine National Exchange Bank of Milwaukee objected, for the reason that the question called for a legal conclusion, which objection was overruled, and said Marine National Exchange Bank of Milwaukee then and there excepted. The witness answered that until the 31st day of January, 1930, Hackett, Hoff & Thiermann, Inc., had sufficient bonds in its possession, as is shown by Exhibit 7 of said Exhibit 2. After that date, Hackett, Hoff & Thiermann, Inc.,

did not have sufficient unpledged bonds in its possession at
any time to retire the first mortgage. The objection of the
Marine National Exchange Bank of Milwaukee to the
81 question was renewed, and the West Side Bank joined
in said objection. Said objections were overruled, and
an exception was then and there taken.

Cross-Examination by Marine National Exchange Bank of Milwaukee.

"Exhibit 1 of Kalt-Zimmers Exhibit 2 shows that bonds
amounting to $18,500.00 of the Kalt-Zimmers Manufacturing
Company were pledged to sundry banks. The record does not
show whether more bonds were pledged at any one time, but
only the bonds pledged as collateral as of the date of the adjudication of bankruptcy of Hackett, Hoff & Thiermann, Inc.
The general ledger of Hackett, Hoff & Thiermann, Inc., was
the source of the information contained in Exhibit 4 of said
Exhibit 2. In preparing said exhibit, I took into consideration
general voucher number 1768 which is now shown to me."
Said voucher was received in evidence and marked "KALT-
ZIMMERS EXHIBIT 3", said exhibit being a journal voucher
of Hackett, Hoff & Thiermann, Inc., showing a credit to Kalt-
Zimmers Manufacturing Company on October 31, 1929, for the
sum of $115,000.00. "The entry for the voucher was also
made in the accounts payable ledger of Hackett, Hoff & Thiermann, Inc., under the same date." The ledger sheet mentioned was received in evidence and marked "KALT-ZIM-
MERS EXHIBIT 4." "Said Exhibit 4 shows the payments
made from time to time for the benefit of Kalt-Zimmers Manufacturing Company. The balance of the account is $25,000
which was due from Hackett, Hoff & Thiermann, Inc., to Kalt-
Zimmers. The private ledger of Hackett, Hoff & Thiermann,
Inc., contains a record of the sales, repurchases and resales
of the bonds of Kalt-Zimmers Manufacturing Company but
does not include a record of the pledge of the bonds. Exhibit 4 of Kalt-Zimmers Manufacturing Company Exhibit 2
shows an original debit of $115,000 in favor of Kalt-
82 Zimmers. Some of the bonds pledged to the Marine National Exchange Bank of Milwaukee and the West Side
Bank had been previously sold by Hackett, Hoff & Thiermann, Inc., and were subsequently repurchased by it and
later pledged to said banks. The numbers of all of the bonds

sold does not appear in Exhibit 4 of Kalt-Zimmers Exhibit 2.''

Counsel for the Marine National Exchange Bank of Milwaukee produced a book which was identified as the bond record book of Hackett, Hoff & Thiermann, Inc. Said book was marked ''Kalt-Zimmers Exhibit 5.'' ''Kalt-Zimmers Exhibit 5 contains a record of the bonds sold and of the bonds repurchased. This record was not checked in preparing Exhibit 4 of Kalt-Zimmers Exhibit 2, and there might be some bonds that were sold and repurchased prior to the date of the audit. Exhibit 4 of said Exhibit 2 would not reflect all of the sales by third parties to Hackett, Hoff & Thiermann, Inc.''

''Exhibit 5 of Kalt-Zimmers Exhibit 2 shows the current account of Kalt-Zimmers with Hackett, Hoff & Thiermann, Inc., according to the books of the latter. It shows an original credit to Kalt-Zimmers of $115,000.00 with various debits entered and a credit balance on July 21, 1931, amounting to $25,000.00 and bonds in the possession of Hackett, Hoff & Thiermann, Inc., on said date amounting to $6,500.00. In addition, there were at that time pledged to the Marine National Exchange Bank of Milwaukee and to the West Side Bank bonds amounting to $14,500.00, and bonds amounting to $4,000.00 were pledged to secure a personal loan of Max L. Thiermann.''

KALT-ZIMMERS EXHIBIT 5 was received in evidence. A portion of said exhibit was marked ''KALT-ZIMMERS EXHIBIT 6'' and was received in evidence. The referee directed that Exhibits 3, 4, 5 and 6, being books of Hackett, Hoff & Thiermann, Inc., remain in the custody of the trustee.

83   ''Bond No. 99 of the Kalt-Zimmers Manufacturing Company was not previously sold by Hackett, Hoff & Thiermann, Inc. Bonds No. 100, 113, and 116 were previously sold and repurchased by Hackett, Hoff & Thiermann, Inc. Bonds No. 119, 120, 121, 122, 123, 124, 125 and 138 had not been sold by Hackett, Hoff & Thiermann, Inc., before they were pledged to the Marine National Exchange Bank of Milwaukee.''

Cross-Examination by West Side Bank.

''Exhibit 4 of Kalt-Zimmers Exhibit 2 shows that bond No. 62 for $1,000.00 was originally sold by Hackett, Hoff & Thiermann, Inc., on January 9, 1930. The sales invoices of Hackett, Hoff & Thiermann, Inc., show that the bonds mentioned was sold on that date to Armin F. Gerlach. Also the record shows that bonds No. 66, 72, 73 and 74, each of the par value of $1,000.00, were sold by Hackett, Hoff & Thiermann, Inc., and subsequently repurchased. The records do not show that bonds No. 94, 95, 96, 110, 128, 129 and 130 were previously sold. Over all the period covered by the transactions, there was a credit to Kalt-Zimmers shown upon the books of Hackett, Hoff & Thiermann, Inc., in a sum of not less than $25,-000.00.''

MR. JOHN B. CASPER was then called as a witness by the Kalt-Zimmers Manufacturing Company and testified as follows:

Direct Examination.

''I am the Secretary of the Kalt-Zimmers Manufacturing Company. The witness then produced a statement of an account of Hackett, Hoff & Thiermann, Inc., to Kalt-Zimmers.'' The statement was marked ''KALT-ZIMMERS EXHIBIT 7'' and was received in evidence. ''The statement was received by Kalt-Zimmers Manufacturing Company on or about June 9, 1930. The correction appearing on the statement was made by myself at the office of Hackett, Hoff & Thiermann, Inc.'' Said exhibit is in words and figures as follows:

84

Milwaukee, Wisconsin, June 9, 1930.

Hackett, Hoff & Thiermann, Inc.

To Kalt-Zimmers Manufacturing Co., Dr.

8-15-29	Ref. 1st M'tge Bonds	$115,000.00		
	Less—bonds held for retirement of prior m'tge	30,000.00		
	Bonds issued		$85,000.00	
11-26-29	Allen Bradley Co. bds	5,000.00		
	Fairmount Riding Academy bds	3,000.00		
	Treselro Realty Co. bds	2,000.00		
			10,000.00	$95,000.00
8-15-29	Commission loan $85,000	4,250.00		
	Legal services	500.00		
	Abstract extensions	53.50		
	Cert. copy of Art. of Inc.	8.40		
	Bond forms and printing	163.16		
	Revenue stamps	57.50		
	Recording trust mortgage	7.60		
	Appraisals	190.00		
	Filing fees	67.50		
	Engineer fees	25.00		
	Maps and survey	15.00		
			5,337.66	
	Insurance account	279.74		

2-15-30	Interest	726.38		
	2% federal tax at source..............	69.00		
			795.38	
11-2-29	E. Brielmaier & Sons Co..............	2,400.00		
1-10-30	"	1,000.00		
			3,400.00	
11-11-29	H. Schmidtt & Sons....................	6,000.00		
11-14	"	3,071.16		
11-22	"	3,000.00		
12-10	"	20,000.00		
12-14	"	3,205.00		
1-10-30	"	10,982.54		
2-11	"	6,533.80		
4-10	"	5,193.79		
			57,986.29	
11-20-29	Wenzel & Hennoch Co.................	1,564.85		
12-20	"	1,530.00		
1-20-30	"	1,020.00		
3-27	"	1,236.80		
			5,351.65	
85 12-21-29	Jos. L. Wittig Co.................$	2,000.00		
1-20-30	"	4,000.00		
3-27-30	"	1,716.21		
				$ 7,716.21
1-10-30	Mil. Ornamental Plaster Co...........	3,000.00		
3-20	"	794.00		
			3,794.00	
1-20-30	U. K. Electric Co.....................	1,000.00		
3-27	"	350.00		
			1,350.00	
1-20-30	Grinell Co.	1,700.00		
2-20-30	"	795.83		
			2,495.83	
1-21-20	S. Heller Elevator....................	3,700.00		
3-1-30	"	697.00		
			4,397.00	
3-21-30	H. F. Haessler Hdw. Co...............		4.00	
4-2-30	Midwest Ventilating Works............	6.85		
5-12	"	99.96		
			106.81	
4-22-30	Globe Wire & Iron Works.............		196.00	
				$93,210.57
				1,789.43

Cross-Examination by Marine National Exchange Bank of Milwaukee.

"I had previously received a statement of account from Hackett, Hoff & Thiermann, Inc., but I do not have that statement with me. The statement produced is a corrected statement." The Counsel for the Marine National Exchange Bank of Milwaukee produced a copy of a statement of Hackett, Hoff & Thiermann, Inc., to Kalt-Zimmers Manufacturing Company, dated February 10, 1930. The statement was marked "Kalt-Zimmers Exhibit 8" and was shown to the witness. "I may have the original of the statement in my file, but if I received the same and made objection to the items, the statement might have been left with Mr. Thiermann for corrections. There was some question raised as to some of the charges, such as the charge for legal services."

The counsel for the Marine National Exchange Bank of Milwaukee produced a copy of an instrument purporting to be an underwriting agreement between the Kalt-Zimmers 86   Manufacturing Company and Hackett, Hoff & Thiermann, Inc. It was then stipulated that no objection would be made on the ground that the instrument was a copy of the original agreement. Said agreement was marked "Kalt-Zimmers Exhibit 9" and was offered in evidence, whereupon the following proceedings were had:

"By Mr. Fish: I object to it—if it varies the terms of the trust deed subsequently executed, it is not competent. It is a prior writing before the trust deed.

(Discussion off the record)

By Mr. Fish: I object if it tends to add to or vary the terms of the trust indenture.

By the Referee: I don't understand the purpose of offering it.

By Mr. Kaumheimer: The purpose is to show a loan of $115,000 based on the issuance of these bonds. The agreement agrees to loan $115,000 in exchange for the bonds. Furthermore it shows that the bonds were to be issued to Hackett, Hoff & Thiermann in exchange for that amount of money, less certain commissions and other things. Furthermore, that interest is to be computed and paid on amounts as drawn. That does not appear anywhere in the trust indenture. It shows also relationship of underwriter and borrower, between Hackett, Hoff & Thiermann and Kalt-Zimmers Manufacturing Company, and I think in that respect it is pertinent.

(Discussion off the record)

By Mr. Fish: I feel it is immaterial. You probably don't want to argue it out now.

(Discussion off the record)

By the Referee: I will receive it subject to the objection of Kalt-Zimmers Manufacturing Company. I am too unfamiliar with the trust indenture to make a definite ruling I think."

Said EXHIBIT NO. 9 was in words and figures as follows:

Milwaukee, Wisconsin.
August 31, 1929.

Kalt-Zimmers Mfg. Company,
    Milwaukee, Wisconsin.

87 Gentlemen:

We hereby propose to loan to you the sum of One Hundred Fifteen Thousand Dollars ($115,000.00) to bear interest at the rate of six per cent (6%) per annum, payable semi-annually, the payment of which is to be secured by a refunding first trust mortgage of property known and described as follows:

Lots numbered one (1), two (2), three (3) and four (4), Block numbered five (5) in Milwaukee Proper, being Lot numbered four (4) of fractional section 32, Township 7 North, Range 22 East, the Fifth Ward of the City and County of Milwaukee, Wisconsin.

Said trust mortgage shall also cover the rents, issues and profits of the premises.

The trust mortgage is to run for a term of ten (10) years and the bonds are to mature serially and to be payable as follows:

Aug. 15, 1930, $5000	Aug. 15, 1935, $5000
Aug. 15, 1931, 5000	Aug. 15, 1936, 5000
Aug. 15, 1932, 5000	Aug. 15, 1937, 5000
Aug. 15, 1933, 5000	Aug. 15, 1938, 5000
Aug. 15, 1934, 5000	Aug. 15, 1939, 70000

The trust mortgage is to be executed by you to Hackett, Hoff & Thiermann, Incorporated, as Trustee, for the benefit of the eventual holders of the bonds and its own benefit under this underwriting agreement.

The bonds and trust mortgage securing same ar to be in the usual form prescribed by us.

You are to pay us a commission of five per cent (5%) on the principal amount of the loan if made, and it is understood that you are to pay in addition thereto, whether a Class "A" permit therefor is granted by the Railroad Commission of Wisconsin or not, all expenses incurred in making this bond issue, such as extensions of abstract, drawing of papers, legal services, recording papers, revenue stamps, printing of bonds, traveling, permit to sell bonds, surety bond or personal bonds, appraisals, and any other expenses which may be incurred by reason of this loan.

It is agreed, and the trust mortgage will provide, that all fire, tornado, plate glass, boiler explosion, workmen's compensation, liability and other kinds of insurance whatsoever carried by you, or required by the Trustee, shall be written in companies selected by the Trustee and placed through agencies or underwriters selected by the Trustee.

You agree that you will, when required, execute separate or additional mortgages covering any part of the real estate or any items of personal property or equipment intended to be mortgaged, and also any after-acquired items of personal property, and that we may require you to execute additional real estate or chattel mortgages covering such real or personal property at any time after the building is completed and the personal property equipment installed so as to cover and mortgage all such personal property for the benefit of the bondholders.

88   It is also understood and agreed that if you desire to call Five Thousand Dollars ($5,000.00) or more of the bonds before maturity, you may do so at any interest payment date by giving sixty (60) days notice in writing to the Trustee and by paying a premium of one per cent (1%) to the bondholders.

It is also understood that interest is to be computed and paid on amounts as drawn.

All payments of principal and interest to be made by you not less than five (5) days prior to the date of such payments becoming due.

The bonds shall be signed by the president and secretary of your corporation and certified to by the Trustee and delivered to the undersigned, and the undersigned shall pay out of the proceeds of the bond issue sufficient money to satisfy the mortgage now encumbering the property above described; the balance of the proceeds shall then be used to pay for the construction of the building to be erected, after you have expended and invested in the construction of the new building, such an amount of money that the net proceeds of the bond issue will be sufficient to pay all the remaining cost of the building, so that when the proceeds of the bond issue are fully disbursed, the building will be entirely completed and paid for.

When you have paid out and disbursed such a sum of money that the proceeds of the bond issue, less charges and commission, will pay the balance of such cost, then the money in our hands is to be disbursed toward the cost of the building on architect's certificate approved by you, as the building progresses to completion, and on receipt by us of proper waivers of mechanics' liens. The trust mortgage is to be at all times a first and prior lien on the lands and building.

The plans and specifications for the new building and also all contracts for or pertaining to the erection thereof and all prices proposed to be paid for the erection and completion of such building must be submitted to use for approval before any money is drawn.

No changes of such plans and specifications, either by way of elimination or extras, shall be made without our approval before any liabilities hereunder are incurred by you.

You are to furnish complete abstract of title showing good, unencumbered, marketable title to your property in you, and to furnish us with current tax receipts to date.

You are to procure from the Railroad Commission of Wisconsin a permit authorizing us to sell these bonds as Class "A" securities in the State of Wisconsin, and it is understood that this agreement is conditioned on the securing of such permit for the full amount of such bonds to be issued hereunder.

In case of your acceptance of this proposition, it is agreed that the relations herein contemplated between you and us exist, and that any agreements or other instruments executed by you to us may be accepted and held by us in pursuant of this general agreement and for the benefit of the eventual

89   holders of the bonds to be secured by such trust mortgage, even though the same, in execution, ante-date such last named bonds and trust mortgage.

If the above terms are acceptable to you, kindly return one copy of this agreemnet signed and oblige.

Yours very truly,
By W. F. KEMKE
Vice-President.

GK

The foregoing proposition is accepted this 9th day of October, 1929, and Hackett, Hoff & Thiermann, Incorporated, is authorized to have the trust mortgage drawn, bonds printed, abstract extended and title examined, all at our expense.

KALT-ZIMMERS MFG. COMPANY,
By JOHN B. CASPER.

Cross-Examination by West Side Bank.

"The Kalt-Zimmers Manufacturing Company had a set of books which recorded the transactions with Hackett, Hoff & Thiermann, Inc. There is no account in the books showing the amount due from Hackett, Hoff & Thiermann, Inc."

Redirect Examination.

"The ledger of Kalt-Zimmers Manufacturing Company has an account entitled 'New Building Addition', and that account shows a bond issue of $85,000 by Hackett, Hoff & Thiermann, Inc. In addition, the account shows an item of $10,000 paid to Hackett, Hoff & Thiermann, Inc." The Kalt-Zimmers Manufacturing Company then offered in evidence ledger page 26A entitled "New Building Addition" to which the counsel for the Marine National Exchange Bank of Milwaukee objected on the ground that the same was not communicated to Hackett, Hoff & Thiermann, Inc., and that the witness was not qualified to verify said account. The Referee sustained the objection, to which ruling the Kalt-Zimmers Manufacturing Company duly excepted. "Account No. 12 of the same ledger entitled 'Mortgage Bonds to Hackett, Hoff & Thiermann, Inc.; on New Building' contains an entry of a bond loan amounting to $85,000. I transacted the business with Hackett, Hoff & Thiermann, Inc., and know that the entry is correct. The entry was made in the books from memoranda which I gave the bookkeeper." The account was 90 received in evidence over the objection of the Marine National Exchange Bank and the West Side Bank that said account was not properly verified, to which ruling of the Referee an exception was then and there taken.

Recross Examination of Marine National Exchange Bank of Milwaukee.

"I signed and executed bonds of the face value of $155,000 of the first refunding mortgage bond issue and delivered the same to Hackett, Hoff & Thiermann, Inc. I believe that the bonds were certified by Hackett, Hoff & Thiermann, Inc., as trustee. The seal of Kalt-Zimmers Manufacturing Company was also affixed to the bonds and the coupons signed with the facsimile signature of the officers.''

REBUTTAL TESTIMONY OF MARINE NATIONAL EXCHANGE BANK OF MILWAUKEE.

M. H. GROSSMAN was then called as a witness by the Marine National Exchange Bank of Milwaukee and testified as follows:

Direct Examination.

''I am the Trustee in Bankruptcy of Hackett, Hoff & Thiermann, Inc., and prior to 1931 I was in the investment banking business. I was in such business in Milwaukee, Wisconsin, since 1907, and I am familiar with the custom prevailing between banks and underwriting houses in the City of Milwaukee as to collateral loans.'' The following proceedings were then had:

''Q. Will you state whether or not it was the general practice and custom among underwriting houses in the City of Milwaukee, in the years that I have mentioned, (1929, 1930 and 1931) to pledge bonds to banks upon the underwriting of securities?

By Mr. Fish: Objected to as incompetent.

(Discussion off the record)

By the Referee: Overruled.

　　Exception.

A. Yes.

By Mr. Marshutz: I move to strike that out as immaterial. There has been no showing in this case that there was
91　any underwriting of these bonds at all.

　　By the Referee: It may stand.

　　Exception.

Q. Was the same true in cases where the house purchasing the bonds and selling the same was also the trustee under the terms of the trust mortgage?

By Mr. Fish: Objected to as immaterial and incompetent.

By the Referee: Objection overruled.

　　Exception.

A. The very nature of the bond business is such that they need to hypothecate the bonds they buy in order to pay for them.

Q. So your answer would be 'Yes'?

A. My answer would be 'Yes'.''

ARTHUR H. LINDSAY was then called as a witness by the Marine National Exchange Bank of Milwaukee and testified as follows:

Direct Examination.

"I am the Chairman of the Board of the Marine National Exchange Bank of Milwaukee. I have held that position for a little over two years. Prior to that time I was the President of the Marine National Bank of Milwaukee and have been in the banking business in the City of Milwaukee since 1878. I am familiar with the custom and practice of banks in the City of Milwaukee during the years 1929, 1930 and 1931." The following proceedings were then had:

"Q. Was the general custom and practice of banks doing business in Milwaukee in 1929, 1930 and 1931, to loan money to investment houses and bond houses, receiving as collateral the bonds purchased by such houses?

By Mr. Marshutz: Objected to as incompetent and immaterial.

By the Referee: Objection overruled.

Exception.

A. To the best of my knowledge, it was.

Q. Was it the custom and practice of banks located in the City of Milwaukee, in the years 1929, 1930 and 1931, to 92 loan money to underwriting houses, which also acted as trustee of the bond issue in question, and to receive such bonds as collateral?

By Mr. Fish: Same objection as before.

By the Referee: Same ruling.

Exception.

A. To the best of my knowledge it was."

Thereupon the proceeding was adjourned unto Friday, October 21, 1932, at 10:00 o'clock A. M., at which time the proceeding continued.

JOHN M. CASPER was then recalled for further cross-examination and testified as follows:

"Kalt-Zimmers Exhibit 8 is a copy of a statement received by Kalt-Zimmers Manufacturing Company from Hackett, Hoff & Thiermann, Inc." The original of said statement was marked "Kalt-Zimmers Exhibit 8A". KALT-ZIMMERS EXHIBIT 8 and 8A were offered in evidence and objection was made thereto on the ground that said statements are incompetent, irrelevant and immaterial. The Referee overruled the objection, to which ruling Kalt-Zimmers Manufacturing Company then and there excepted. Said EXHIBIT 8 is in the words and figures as follows:

Milwaukee, Wisc., Feb. 10th, 1930.

Hackett, Hoff & Thiermann, Inc.,
    To Kalt-Zimmers Manufacturing Co.,

8/15/29	First Mortgage Ref. Gold Bonds		115,000.00	
11/26	Allen-Bradley Co. Bds. #582/586 Incl.	5,000.00		
	Fairmount Rid. Academy Bds. 1/3 "	3,000.00		
	Treselro Rlty. Co., Bds. 262,264/266 ..	2,000.00	10,000.00	
1/2/30	Treselro Rlty. Co., Bds. 261,263		1,000.00	126,000.00
	Loan Expenses			
8/15/29	Commission Loan 5%	5,750.00		
	Legal Services	500.00		
	Abstracts	53.50		
	Cert. copies Art. of Inc.	8.40		
	Bond Print. & Forms	163.16		
	Revenue stamps	57.50		
93	Rec. Trust deed	7.60		
	Appraisals	100.00		
	Filing fee	67.50		
	Engineers fee	25.00		
	Maps & Surveys	15.00	6,837.66	
	Contractors			
11/2/29	E. Brielmaier & Sons Co.	2,400.00		
1/10/30	" "	1,000.00	3,400.00	
11/11/29	H. Schmitt & Son	6,000.00		
11/14	" "	3,071.16		
11/22	" "	3,000.00		
12/10	" "	20,000.00		
12/14	" "	3,205.00		
1/10130	" "	10,982.54	46,258.70	
11/20/29	Wenzel & Henoch Co.	1,564.85		
12/20	" "	1,530.00		
1/20/30	" "	1,020.00	4,114.85	
12/21/29	Jos. L. Wittig Co.	2,000.00		
1/20/30	" "	4,000.00	6,000.00	
1/10/30	Mil. Ornamental Plast.		3,000.00	
1/20	U. K. Elect. Co.		1,000.00	
1/20	Grinnel Co.		1,700.00	
1/21	S. Heller Elev. Co.		3,700.00	76,011.21
	Balance			49,088.79

The counsel for the Marine National Exchange Bank of Milwaukee produced a statement of Hackett, Hoff & Thiermann, Inc., dated June 9, 1930. The statement was marked "Kalt-Zimmers Exhibit 11". "The exhibit was received by

(Bond) No. 94 $15.00   (Coupon) No. 18

On the 15th day of Aug. 1938
Kalt-Zimmers Manufacturing Company
will pay to the bearer hereof at the office of
Hackett, Hoff & Thiermann, Incorporated,
Milwaukee, Wisconsin, Trustee,
Fifteen and No/100 Dollars ($15.00)
in gold coin of the United States of America of or equal to
the present standard of weight and fineness, being six (6)
months' interest on its six per cent refunding first mortgage
serial gold bond, subject, however, to the conditions of said
bond, unless said bond shall have been previously redeemed
or called for redemption under the provisions of the trust
mortgage securing the same, and payment provided therefor.

KALT-ZIMMERS MANUFACTURING COMPANY,
By JOHN B. CASPER
Treasurer.

(Bond) No. 94 $15.00   (Coupon) No. 17

On the 15th day of Feb. 1938
Kalt-Zimmers Manufacturing Company
will pay to the bearer hereof at the office of
Hackett, Hoff & Thiermann, Incorporated,
Milwaukee, Wisconsin, Trustee,
Fifteen and No/100 Dollars ($15.00)
in gold coin of the United States of America of or equal to
the present standard of weight and fineness, being six (6)
months' interest on its six per cent refunding first mortgage
serial gold bond, subject, however, to the conditions of said
bond, unless said bond shall have been previously redeemed
or called for redemption under the provisions of the trust
mortgage securing the same, and payment provided therefor.

KALT-ZIMMERS MANUFACTURING COMPANY,
By JOHN B. CASPER
Treasurer.

(Bond) No. 94 $15.00   (Coupon) No. 16

On the 15th day of Aug. 1937
Kalt-Zimmers Manufacturing Company
will pay to the bearer hereof at the office of
Hackett, Hoff & Thiermann, Incorporated,
Milwaukee, Wisconsin, Trustee,
Fifteen and No/100 Dollars ($15.00)
in gold coin of the United States of America of or equal to
the present standard of weight and fineness, being six (6)
months' interest on its six per cent refunding first mortgage
serial gold bond, subject, however, to the conditions of said
bond, unless said bond shall have been previously redeemed
or called for redemption under the provisions of the trust
mortgage securing the same, and payment provided therefor.

KALT-ZIMMERS MANUFACTURING COMPANY,
By JOHN B. CASPER
Treasurer.

(Bond) No. 94 $15.00   (Coupon) No. 15

On the 15th day of Feb. 1937
Kalt-Zimmers Manufacturing Company
will pay to the bearer hereof at the office of
Hackett, Hoff & Thiermann, Incorporated,
Milwaukee, Wisconsin, Trustee,
Fifteen and No/100 Dollars ($15.00)
in gold coin of the United States of America of or equal to
the present standard of weight and fineness, being six (6)
months' interest on its six per cent refunding first mortgage
serial gold bond, subject, however, to the conditions of said
bond, unless said bond shall have been previously redeemed
or called for redemption under the provisions of the trust
mortgage securing the same, and payment provided therefor.

KALT-ZIMMERS MANUFACTURING COMPANY,
By JOHN B. CASPER
Treasurer.

(Bond) No. 94 $15.00   (Coupon) No. 14

On the 15th day of Aug. 1936
Kalt-Zimmers Manufacturing Company
will pay to the bearer hereof at the office of
Hackett, Hoff & Thiermann, Incorporated,
Milwaukee, Wisconsin, Trustee,
Fifteen and No/100 Dollars ($15.00)
in gold coin of the United States of America of or equal to
the present standard of weight and fineness, being six (6)
months' interest on its six per cent refunding first mortgage
serial gold bond, subject, however, to the conditions of said
bond, unless said bond shall have been previously redeemed
or called for redemption under the provisions of the trust
mortgage securing the same, and payment provided therefor.

KALT-ZIMMERS MANUFACTURING COMPANY,
By JOHN B. CASPER
Treasurer.

(Bond) No. 94 $15.00   (Coupon) No. 13

On the 15th day of Feb. 1936
Kalt-Zimmers Manufacturing Company
will pay to the bearer hereof at the office of
Hackett, Hoff & Thiermann, Incorporated,
Milwaukee, Wisconsin, Trustee,
Fifteen and No/100 Dollars ($15.00)
in gold coin of the United States of America of or equal to
the present standard of weight and fineness, being six (6)
months' interest on its six per cent refunding first mortgage
serial gold bond, subject, however, to the conditions of said
bond, unless said bond shall have been previously redeemed
or called for redemption under the provisions of the trust
mortgage securing the same, and payment provided therefor.

KALT-ZIMMERS MANUFACTURING COMPANY,
By JOHN B. CASPER
Treasurer.

(Bond) No. 94 $15.00   (Coupon) No. 12

On the 15th day of Aug. 1935
Kalt-Zimmers Manufacturing Company
will pay to the bearer hereof at the office of
Hackett, Hoff & Thiermann, Incorporated,
Milwaukee, Wisconsin, Trustee,
Fifteen and No/100 Dollars ($15.00)
in gold coin of the United States of America of or equal to
the present standard of weight and fineness, being six (6)
months' interest on its six per cent refunding first mortgage
serial gold bond, subject, however, to the conditions of said
bond, unless said bond shall have been previously redeemed
or called for redemption under the provisions of the trust
mortgage securing the same, and payment provided therefor.

KALT-ZIMMERS MANUFACTURING COMPANY,
By JOHN B. CASPER
Treasurer.

(Bond) No. 94   · $15.00   (Coupon) No. 11

On the 15th day of Feb. 1935
Kalt-Zimmers Manufacturing Company
will pay to the bearer hereof at the office of
Hackett, Hoff & Thiermann, Incorporated,
Milwaukee, Wisconsin, Trustee,
Fifteen and No/100 Dollars ($15.00)
in gold coin of the United States of America of or equal to
the present standard of weight and fineness, being six (6)
months' interest on its six per cent refunding first mortgage
serial gold bond, subject, however, to the conditions of said
bond, unless said bond shall have been previously redeemed
or called for redemption under the provisions of the trust
mortgage securing the same, and payment provided therefor.

KALT-ZIMMERS MANUFACTURING COMPANY,
By JOHN B. CASPER
Treasurer.

ARTHUR H. LINDSAY was then called as a witness by the Marine National Exchange Bank of Milwaukee and testified as follows:

Direct Examination.

"I am the Chairman of the Board of the Marine National Exchange Bank of Milwaukee. I have held that position for a little over two years. Prior to that time I was the President of the Marine National Bank of Milwaukee and have been in the banking business in the City of Milwaukee since 1878. I am familiar with the custom and practice of banks in the City of Milwaukee during the years 1929, 1930 and 1931." The following proceedings were then had:

"Q. Was the general custom and practice of banks doing business in Milwaukee in 1929, 1930 and 1931, to loan money to investment houses and bond houses, receiving as collateral the bonds purchased by such houses?

By Mr. Marshutz: Objected to as incompetent and immaterial.

By the Referee: Objection overruled.

Exception.

A. To the best of my knowledge, it was.

Q. Was it the custom and practice of banks located in the City of Milwaukee, in the years 1929, 1930 and 1931, to
92 loan money to underwriting houses, which also acted as trustee of the bond issue in question, and to receive such bonds as collateral?

By Mr. Fish: Same objection as before.

By the Referee: Same ruling.

Exception.

A. To the best of my knowledge it was."

Thereupon the proceeding was adjourned unto Friday, October 21, 1932, at 10:00 o'clock A. M., at which time the proceeding continued.

JOHN M. CASPER was then recalled for further cross-examination and testified as follows:

"Kalt-Zimmers Exhibit 8 is a copy of a statement received by Kalt-Zimmers Manufacturing Company from Hackett, Hoff & Thiermann, Inc." The original of said statement was marked "Kalt-Zimmers Exhibit 8A". KALT-ZIMMERS EXHIBIT 8 and 8A were offered in evidence and objection was made thereto on the ground that said statements are incompetent, irrelevant and immaterial. The Referee overruled the objection, to which ruling Kalt-Zimmers Manufacturing Company then and there excepted. Said EXHIBIT 8 is in the words and figures as follows:

Milwaukee, Wisc., Feb. 10th, 1930.

Hackett, Hoff & Thiermann, Inc.,
   To Kalt-Zimmers Manufacturing Co.,

8/15/29	First Mortgage Ref. Gold Bonds.............		115,000.00	
11/26	Allen-Bradley Co. Bds. #582/586 Incl.	5,000.00		
	Fairmount Rid. Academy Bds. 1/3 "	3,000.00		
	Treselro Rlty. Co., Bds. 262,264/266..	2,000.00	10,000.00	
1/2/30	Treselro Rlty. Co., Bds. 261,263......		1,000.00	126,000.00
	Loan Expenses			
8/15/29	Commission Loan 5%...............	5,750.00		
	Legal Services	500.00		
	Abstracts	53.50		
	Cert. copies Art. of Inc...........	8.40		
	Bond Print. & Forms..............	163.16		
	Revenue stamps	57.50		
93	Rec. Trust deed	7.60		
	Appraisals	190.00		
	Filing fee	67.50		
	Engineers fee	25.00		
	Maps & Surveys	15.00	6,837.66	
	Contractors			
11/2/29	E. Brielmaier & Sons Co.............	2,400.00		
1/10/30	" "	1,000.00	3,400.00	
11/11/29	H. Schmitt & Son.................	6,000.00		
11/14	" "	3,071.16		
11/22	" "	3,000.00		
12/10	" "	20,000.00		
12/14	" "	3,205.00		
1/10/30	" "	10,982.54	46,258.70	
11/20/29	Wenzel & Henoch Co...............	1,564.85		
12/20	" "	1,530.00		
1/20/30	" "	1,020.00	4,114.85	
12/21/29	Jos. L. Wittig Co..................	2,000.00		
1/20/30	" "	4,000.00	6,000.00	
1/10/30	Mil. Ornamental Plast..............		3,000.00	
1/20	U. K. Elect. Co....................		1,000.00	
1/20	Grinnel Co.		1,700.00	
1/21	S. Heller Elev. Co.................		3,700.00	76,011.21
	Balance			49,988.79

The counsel for the Marine National Exchange Bank of Milwaukee produced a statement of Hackett, Hoff & Thiermann, Inc., dated June 9, 1930. The statement was marked "Kalt-Zimmers Exhibit 11". "The exhibit was received by

Kalt-Zimmers Manufacturing Company on or about its date. The reason for the variation between Kalt-Zimmers Exhibit 7 and Kalt-Zimmers Exhibit 11 is that Exhibit 11 was received first and contained charges tò which objections were made.''

Redirect Examination.

''The pencil notations on Exhibit 11 are my own memoranda. Upon receipt of Exhibit 11, I went to the office of Hackett, Hoff & Thiermann, Inc., and objected to both the charges for commission and attorneys' fees, and as a result we received Exhibit 7. I also objected to the items contained in Exhibit 8A and was told that corrections would be made.''

94   *Recross Examination.*

''With exception of the two items mentioned, I did not make objections to the items contained on Exhibit 8A, except that it is possible that I called their attention to the credit item of $1,000.''

The above and foregoing is all the evidence introduced at the trial of said matter and all proceedings had in the trial thereof.

Wherefore, the appellants, Marine National Exchange Bank of Milwaukee, and West Side Bank, pray that the above statement of evidence be settled, approved and allowed by the above entitled court as a true, full, correct and complete statement of all the evidence taken and given on the trial of said cause for use on the appeal taken to the Circuit Court of Appeals for the Seventh Circuit.

Dated this 18th day of July, A. D. 1933.

LEON E. KAUMHEIMER
DOUGLASS VAN DYKE
Attorneys for appellant, Marine National Exchange Bank of Milwaukee.

GEORGE A. AFFELDT
Attorney for appellant, West Side Bank.

The foregoing statement of Summary of Evidence is in all respects hereby approved and settled as a true and complete summary of the evidence adduced on the hearing of the above entitled matter.

Dated this 28 day of July, 1933.

F. A. GEIGER
United States District Judge.

95   WEST SIDE EXHIBIT C 6.

(Coupons)

(Bond) No. 94 $15.00   (Coupon) No. 20

On the 15th day of Aug. 1939
Kalt-Zimmers Manufacturing Company
will pay to the bearer hereof at the office of
Hackett, Hoff & Thiermann, Incorporated,
Milwaukee, Wisconsin, Trustee,
Fifteen and No/100 Dollars ($15.00)
in gold coin of the United States of America of or equal to
the present standard of weight and fineness, being six (6)
months' interest on its six per cent refunding first mortgage
serial gold bond, subject, however, to the conditions of said
bond, unless said bond shall have been previously redeemed
or called for redemption under the provisions of the trust
mortgage securing the same, and payment provided therefor.

KALT-ZIMMERS MANUFACTURING COMPANY,
By JOHN B. CASPER
Treasurer.

(Bond) No. 94 $15.00   (Coupon) No. 19

On the 15th day of Feb. 1939
Kalt-Zimmers Manufacturing Company
will pay to the bearer hereof at the office of
Hackett, Hoff & Thiermann, Incorporated,
Milwaukee, Wisconsin, Trustee,
Fifteen and No/100 Dollars ($15.00)
in gold coin of the United States of America of or equal to
the present standard of weight and fineness, being six (6)
months' interest on its six per cent refunding first mortgage
serial gold bond, subject, however, to the conditions of said
bond, unless said bond shall have been previously redeemed
or called for redemption under the provisions of the trust
mortgage securing the same, and payment provided therefor.

KALT-ZIMMERS MANUFACTURING COMPANY,
By JOHN B. CASPER
Treasurer.

(Bond) No. 94 $15.00   (Coupon) No. 18

On the 15th day of Aug. 1938
Kalt-Zimmers Manufacturing Company
will pay to the bearer hereof at the office of
Hackett, Hoff & Thiermann, Incorporated,
Milwaukee, Wisconsin, Trustee,
Fifteen and No/100 Dollars ($15.00)
in gold coin of the United States of America of or equal to
the present standard of weight and fineness, being six (6)
months' interest on its six per cent refunding first mortgage
serial gold bond, subject, however, to the conditions of said
bond, unless said bond shall have been previously redeemed
or called for redemption under the provisions of the trust
mortgage securing the same, and payment provided therefor.

KALT-ZIMMERS MANUFACTURING COMPANY,
By JOHN B. CASPER
Treasurer.

(Bond) No. 94 $15.00   (Coupon) No. 17

On the 15th day of Feb. 1938
Kalt-Zimmers Manufacturing Company
will pay to the bearer hereof at the office of
Hackett, Hoff & Thiermann, Incorporated,
Milwaukee, Wisconsin, Trustee,
Fifteen and No/100 Dollars ($15.00)
in gold coin of the United States of America of or equal to
the present standard of weight and fineness, being six (6)
months' interest on its six per cent refunding first mortgage
serial gold bond, subject, however, to the conditions of said
bond, unless said bond shall have been previously redeemed
or called for redemption under the provisions of the trust
mortgage securing the same, and payment provided therefor.

KALT-ZIMMERS MANUFACTURING COMPANY,
By JOHN B. CASPER
Treasurer.

(Bond) No. 94 $15.00 (Coupon) No. 16

On the 15th day of Aug. 1937
Kalt-Zimmers Manufacturing Company
will pay to the bearer hereof at the office of
Hackett, Hoff & Thiermann, Incorporated,
Milwaukee, Wisconsin, Trustee,
Fifteen and No/100 Dollars ($15.00)
in gold coin of the United States of America of or equal to
the present standard of weight and fineness, being six (6)
months' interest on its six per cent refunding first mortgage
serial gold bond, subject, however, to the conditions of said
bond, unless said bond shall have been previously redeemed
or called for redemption under the provisions of the trust
mortgage securing the same, and payment provided therefor.

KALT-ZIMMERS MANUFACTURING COMPANY,
By JOHN B. CASPER
Treasurer.

(Bond) No. 94 $15.00 (Coupon) No. 15

On the 15th day of Feb. 1937
Kalt-Zimmers Manufacturing Company
will pay to the bearer hereof at the office of
Hackett, Hoff & Thiermann, Incorporated,
Milwaukee, Wisconsin, Trustee,
Fifteen and No/100 Dollars ($15.00)
in gold coin of the United States of America of or equal to
the present standard of weight and fineness, being six (6)
months' interest on its six per cent refunding first mortgage
serial gold bond, subject, however, to the conditions of said
bond, unless said bond shall have been previously redeemed
or called for redemption under the provisions of the trust
mortgage securing the same, and payment provided therefor.

KALT-ZIMMERS MANUFACTURING COMPANY,
By JOHN B. CASPER
Treasurer.

(Bond) No. 94 $15.00 (Coupon) No. 14

On the 15th day of Aug. 1936
Kalt-Zimmers Manufacturing Company
will pay to the bearer hereof at the office of
Hackett, Hoff & Thiermann, Incorporated,
Milwaukee, Wisconsin, Trustee,
Fifteen and No/100 Dollars ($15.00)
in gold coin of the United States of America of or equal to
the present standard of weight and fineness, being six (6)
months' interest on its six per cent refunding first mortgage
serial gold bond, subject, however, to the conditions of said
bond, unless said bond shall have been previously redeemed
or called for redemption under the provisions of the trust
mortgage securing the same, and payment provided therefor.

KALT-ZIMMERS MANUFACTURING COMPANY,
By JOHN B. CASPER
Treasurer.

(Bond) No. 94 $15.00 (Coupon) No. 13

On the 15th day of Feb. 1936
Kalt-Zimmers Manufacturing Company
will pay to the bearer hereof at the office of
Hackett, Hoff & Thiermann, Incorporated,
Milwaukee, Wisconsin, Trustee,
Fifteen and No/100 Dollars ($15.00)
in gold coin of the United States of America of or equal to
the present standard of weight and fineness, being six (6)
months' interest on its six per cent refunding first mortgage
serial gold bond, subject, however, to the conditions of said
bond, unless said bond shall have been previously redeemed
or called for redemption under the provisions of the trust
mortgage securing the same, and payment provided therefor.

KALT-ZIMMERS MANUFACTURING COMPANY,
By JOHN B. CASPER
Treasurer.

(Bond) No. 94 $15.00   (Coupon) No. 12

On the 15th day of Aug. 1935
Kalt-Zimmers Manufacturing Company
will pay to the bearer hereof at the office of
Hackett, Hoff & Thiermann, Incorporated,
Milwaukee, Wisconsin, Trustee,
Fifteen and No/100 Dollars ($15.00)
in gold coin of the United States of America of or equal to
the present standard of weight and fineness, being six (6)
months' interest on its six per cent refunding first mortgage
serial gold bond, subject, however, to the conditions of said
bond, unless said bond shall have been previously redeemed
or called for redemption under the provisions of the trust
mortgage securing the same, and payment provided therefor.

KALT-ZIMMERS MANUFACTURING COMPANY,
By JOHN B. CASPER
Treasurer.

(Bond) No. 94   · $15.00   (Coupon) No. 11

On the 15th day of Feb. 1935
Kalt-Zimmers Manufacturing Company
will pay to the bearer hereof at the office of
Hackett, Hoff & Thiermann, Incorporated,
Milwaukee, Wisconsin, Trustee,
Fifteen and No/100 Dollars ($15.00)
in gold coin of the United States of America of or equal to
the present standard of weight and fineness, being six (6)
months' interest on its six per cent refunding first mortgage
serial gold bond, subject, however, to the conditions of said
bond, unless said bond shall have been previously redeemed
or called for redemption under the provisions of the trust
mortgage securing the same, and payment provided therefor.

KALT-ZIMMERS MANUFACTURING COMPANY,
By JOHN B. CASPER
Treasurer.

(Bond) No. 94 $15.00   (Coupon) No. 10

On the 15th day of Aug. 1934
Kalt-Zimmers Manufacturing Company
will pay to the bearer hereof at the office of
Hackett, Hoff & Thiermann, Incorporated,
Milwaukee, Wisconsin, Trustee,
Fifteen and No/100 Dollars ($15.00)
in gold coin of the United States of America of or equal to
the present standard of weight and fineness, being six (6)
months' interest on its six per cent refunding first mortgage
serial gold bond, subject, however, to the conditions of said
bond, unless said bond·shall have been previously redeemed
or called for redemption under the provisions of the trust
mortgage securing the same, and payment provided therefor.

KALT-ZIMMERS MANUFACTURING COMPANY,
By JOHN B. CASPER
Treasurer.

(Bond) No. 94 $15.00   (Coupon) No. 9

On the 15th day of Feb. 1934
Kalt-Zimmers Manufacturing Company
will pay to the bearer hereof at the office of
Hackett, Hoff & Thiermann, Incorporated,
Milwaukee, Wisconsin, Trustee,
Fifteen and No/100 Dollars ($15.00)
in gold coin of the United States of America of or equal to
the present standard of weight and fineness, being six (6)
months' interest on its six per cent refunding first mortgage
serial gold bond, subject, however, to the conditions of said
bond, unless said bond shall have been previously redeemed
or called for redemption under the provisions of the trust
mortgage securing the same, and payment provided therefor.

KALT-ZIMMERS MANUFACTURING COMPANY,
By JOHN B. CASPER
Treasurer.

(Bond) No. 94 $15.00   (Coupon) No. 8

On the 15th day of Aug. 1933
Kalt-Zimmers Manufacturing Company
will pay to the bearer hereof at the office of
Hackett, Hoff & Thiermann, Incorporated,
Milwaukee, Wisconsin, Trustee,
Fifteen and No/100 Dollars ($15.00)
in gold coin of the United States of America of or equal to
the present standard of weight and fineness, being six (6)
months' interest on its six per cent refunding first mortgage
serial gold bond, subject, however, to the conditions of said
bond, unless said bond shall have been previously redeemed
or called for redemption under the provisions of the trust
mortgage securing the same, and payment provided therefor.

KALT-ZIMMERS MANUFACTURING COMPANY,
By JOHN B. CASPER
Treasurer.

(Bond) No. 94 $15.00   (Coupon No. 7

On the 15th day of Feb. 1933
Kalt-Zimmers Manufacturing Company
will pay to the bearer hereof at the office of
Hackett, Hoff & Thiermann, Incorporated,
Milwaukee, Wisconsin, Trustee,
Fifteen and No/100 Dollars ($15.00)
in gold coin of the United States of America of or equal to
the present standard of weight and fineness, being six (6)
months' interest on its six per cent refunding first mortgage
serial gold bond, subject, however, to the conditions of said
bond, unless said bond shall have been previously redeemed
or called for redemption under the provisions of the trust
mortgage securing the same, and payment provided therefor.

KALT-ZIMMERS MANUFACTURING COMPANY,
By JOHN B. CASPER
Treasurer.

(Bond) No. 94 $15.00   (Coupon) No. 6

On the 15th day of Aug. 1932
Kalt-Zimmers Manufacturing Company
will pay to the bearer hereof at the office of
Hackett, Hoff & Thiermann, Incorporated,
Milwaukee, Wisconsin, Trustee,
Fifteen and No/100 Dollars ($15.00)
in gold coin of the United States of America of or equal to
the present standard of weight and fineness, being six (6)
months' interest on its six per cent refunding first mortgage
serial gold bond, subject, however, to the conditions of said
bond, unless said bond shall have been previously redeemed
or called for redemption under the provisions of the trust
mortgage securing the same, and payment provided therefor.

KALT-ZIMMERS MANUFACTURING COMPANY,
By JOHN B. CASPER
Treasurer.

(Bond) No. 94 $15.00   (Coupon) No. 5

On the 15th day of Feb. 1932
Kalt-Zimmers Manufacturing Company
will pay to the bearer hereof at the office of
Hackett, Hoff & Thiermann, Incorporated,
Milwaukee, Wisconsin, Trustee,
Fifteen and No/100 Dollars ($15.00)
in gold coin of the United States of America of or equal to
the present standard of weight and fineness, being six (6)
months' interest on its six per cent refunding first mortgage
serial gold bond, subject, however, to the conditions of said
bond, unless said bond shall have been previously redeemed
or called for redemption under the provisions of the trust
mortgage securing the same, and payment provided therefor.

KALT-ZIMMERS MANUFACTURING COMPANY,
By JOHN B. CASPER
Treasurer.

96   Number 94   (Face of bond)   Dollars 500

UNITED STATES OF AMERICA

STATE OF WISCOSIN

Kalt-Zimmers Manufacturing Company
Milwaukee - Wisconsin

Six Per Cent Refunding

First Mortgage Serial Gold Bond

Kalt-Zimmers Manufacturing Company, of Milwaukee, Wisconsin, (hereinafter referred to as "first party"), a corporation duly organized and existing under and by virtue of the laws of the State of Wisconsin, acknowledges itself to be indebted, and for value received, hereby promises to pay to the bearer hereof, or, if this bond is registered, then to the registered holder hereof, the sum of

Five Hundred Dollars ($500.00)

in gold coin of the United States of America of the present standard of weight and fineness, without grace on the 15th day of August, A. D. 1939, and interest thereon from the 15th day of August, A. D. 1929, at the rate of six per cent (6%) per annum, payable in like gold coin semi-annually on the 15th day of February and August in each year, to the bearer of the properly annexed coupons, on presentation and surrender thereof as they severally become due. Both interest and principal are payable at the office of Hackett, Hoff & Thiermann, Incorporated, Milwaukee, Wisconsin, Trustee. All interest hereon shall be payable without deduction for or on account of any United States income tax which the first party or the Trustee may be required or permitted to pay thereon or retain therefrom by virtue of any present or future law or requirement, except such portion of any such tax in respect of such interest as shall be in excess of two per cent (2%) of such interest in any one year.

This bond is one of a series of duly authorized and issued coupon bonds of said Kalt-Zimmers Manufacturing Company, known as its "Six Per Cent Refunding First Mortgage Serial Gold Bond", numbered consecutively from one (1) to two hundred (200) both inclusive, made by said Kalt-Zimmers Manufacturing Company of like tenor, date and effect, except that seventy (70) of said bonds are of the denomination of One Thousand Dollars ($1,000.00) each, and eighty

(80) of said bonds are of the denomination of Five Hundred Dollars ($500.00) each, and fifty (50) of said bonds are of the denomination of One Hundred Dollars ($100.00) each, aggregating the total principal sum of One Hundred Fifteen Thousand Dollars ($115,000.00), and which bonds mature serially in from one (1) to ten (10) years after date. Said bonds are issued under and secured by a mortgage or deed of trust of even date herewith, duly made, acknowledged and delivered by said Kalt-Zimmers Manufacturing Company to Hackett, Hoff & Thiermann, Incorporated, Trustee, to which deed of trust reference is hereby made with the same effect as though recited at length herein, for the description of the property mortgaged, the nature and extent of the security, the rights of the holders of the bonds, and the terms and conditions upon which the said bonds are issued, held and secured, and may, before their fixed maturities, be declared at once due and payable, and the manner of prepayment before maturity.

This bond shall pass by delivery, except that, after the registration of ownership certified thereon by the transfer agent of the said first party, no transfer shall be valid except upon the books of the transfer agent, unless the last transfer be to bearer, which shall restore transferability by delivery, but this bond shall continue subject to successive registrations and transfers to bearer as aforesaid at the option of each holder. The registry of the bond as above shall not restrain the negotiability of the coupons by delivery.

This bond may be redeemed by said first party prior to maturity, at any interest-payment date, upon payment of the principal hereof, all interest due and accruing to the date of such respective redemption, and, if redemption shall be made before maturity hereof, a premium of one per cent (1%) of the principal hereof, as in said trust deed provided.

In case default shall be made in the payment of interest or principal on said bonds or notes, or either of them, or of the coupons given for such interest, or if any default be made as to any of the covenants or conditions of the deed of trust and remain unrepaired, as therein provided, then the entire principal sum of said bonds or notes, together with all arrearages of interest thereon may be deemed to have become due and payable, as provided in said deed of trust.

In event that any installment of interest on this bond or the principal thereof be not promptly paid as the same becomes due and payable (whether the payment thereof be accelerated or not), any interest or principal so unpaid shall draw interest at the rate of ten per cent (10%) per annum until paid.

This bond shall not be valid for any purpose or be secured

by the said deed of trust unless and until the certificate hereon endorsed be executed by the Trustee under said deed of trust.

Revenue stamps to the amount required by the Internal Revenue Act have been affixed to original Indenture of Mortgage and cancelled.

In Witness Whereof, said Kalt-Zimmers Manufacturing Company has caused these presents to be signed by its president, countersigned by its secretary and its corporate seal to be hereunto affixed, and the interest coupons hereto affixed to be executed in its behalf by the fac-simile signature of its treasurer, this fifteenth day of August, A. D. 1929.

KALT-ZIMMERS MANUFACTURING COMPANY

(Seal)

By OGARITA J. CASPER
President

Countersigned by:
    JOHN B. CASPER
        Secretary.

97   (Endorsement on Bond)
94
United States of America
State of Wisconsin
Kalt-Zimmers Manufacturing Company
Milwaukee, Wisconsin
$500
Refunding First Mortgage Serial Gold Bond
6 Per Cent
Dated August 15, 1929
Due August 15, 1939
Interest Payable February 15 and August 15
Principal and Interest Payable
At the Office of
Hackett, Hoff & Thiermann Incorporated
Milwaukee, Wisconsin
Trustee's Certificate

This is to certify that this bond is one of the bonds mentioned in the mortgage or trust deed referred to within.

HACKETT, HOFF & THIERMANN, INCORPORATED,
Trustee,

By (Signature illegible)
Secretary.

(Notice: No writing on this bond except by Hackett, Hoff & Thiermann, Incorporated, Trustee, or its successor in trust)
Date of Registry   In Whose Name Registered   Registrar

98   Endorsed: * * (Caption) * * Statement of Evidence Lodged July 18, 1933 B. H. Westfahl, Clerk. Service of the within Statement; and the receipt of a copy thereof this 18th day of July, A. D. 1933 is hereby admitted and acknowledged. Filed Jul 28, 1933 B. H. Westfahl, Clerk. I. A. Fish and T. H. Marshutz, Attorneys for Kalt-Zimmers Manufacturing Company, Walter H. Bender and Bender, Trump, McIntyre & Freeman, Attorneys for M. H. Grossman, Esq., Trustee in Bankruptcy.

34   REFEREE'S FINDINGS AND ORDER dated March **D**   11, 1933, filed as follows:

* * (Caption) * *

In the Matter of the Applications of the Marine National Exchange Bank, of Milwaukee, Wisconsin, and The West Side Bank, of Milwaukee, Wisconsin, for Permission to Sell Certain Collateral of the above named Bankrupt held by said Banks as Security for Loans; and the Cross petitions of the Kalt Zimmers Manufacturing Company, a corporation, Objecting to the granting of such Permission and Authority.

In the first instance, the Referee denied jurisdiction of said matter and thereafter upon review of said decision denying jurisdiction it was ordered by the Judge of the United States District Court for the Eastern District of Wisconsin that the Referee hear, and determine, upon notice and upon the merits, the issues raised by said petitions and cross petitions.

The matter of said petitions for right to sell and cross petitions objecting to sale, and the answers of the petitioning banks on behalf of the Marine National Exchange Bank and of the West Side Bank being practically identical as to the purpose, facts, and effect, by stipulation and agreement of all parties concerned said petitions and both of them, and the questions raised thereby, and by the cross petitions and answers, are heard jointly and as one matter and this opinion and order is made jointly and covering the petitions and other pleadings of both petitioning banks.

Said matter was duly heard, at Milwaukee, Wisconsin, on October 17, 1932 and adjourned dates. Testimony was taken, exhibits offered, arguments of counsel heard, and briefs of counsel filed.

The facts in said controversy do not seem to be materially in dispute. Kalt Zimmers Manufacturing Company, 35 agreeable to an "underwriting agreement" executed and delivered to the bankrupt corporation its trust mortgage and first mortgage real estate bonds secured by said trust mortgage in an aggregate amount of One Hundred Fifteen Thousand ($115,000.00) Dollars, duly authenticated and executed. Said trust mortgage contained in effect substantially the usual and ordinary provisions contained in a comprehensive instrument of this kind and in addition thereto two particular provisions:

First, One providing in effect that whereas there was existing upon the mortgaged property at the time of the mortgage in controversy a prior bond issue of Thirty Thousand ($30,000.00) Dollars that the Trustee should retain in trust at all times either bonds of the new issue or the proceeds thereof in an amount equal to the said Thirty Thousand ($30,000.00) Dollars for the purpose of retiring the said remaining Thirty Thousand ($30,000.00) Dollars of the previous issue; and

Second, A provision permitting the Trustee or any of its officers, agents or stockholders to acquire, own and deal in said bonds and coupons with the same right as if not Trustee thereunder, and relieving them of the obligation to account for any profits made thereby.

The bankrupt corporation used certain of said bonds as a deposit in both of the petitioning banks, in some instances as collateral for new loans, and in other instances as substitute collateral for loans upon which the previously existing collateral was simultaneously withdrawn.

Kalt-Zimmers Manufacturing Company questioned the right of the banks to offer said bonds for sale under their collateral note for the alleged reasons, in effect; that said bonds were not negotiable instruments; that said bonds were pledged by the Trustee in Banks in violation of the Uniform Fiduciaries Act of Wisconsin, and that, therefore, the Trustee had no right to pledge and the banks no right to receive; that the banks were not holders in due course 36 and without notice of defect.

Various counsel represented the parties in this controversy and favored the Referee with extremely comprehensive and thorough briefs covering the questions involved. In view of the numerous citations contained in said briefs it would be futile for the Referee to attempt to discuss said briefs and the citations contained therein.

Counsel for the cross petitioner contends that the recitation in the bonds incorporating the trust indenture therein destroys negotiability, and that therefore, the reference thereto should have put the receiving banks upon notice that the Fiduciaries Act had been violated, the trust breached, and that the Trustee had no right to pledge and the bank no right to receive said bonds.

The reference in the bonds to the trust indenture was as follows:

"To which deed of trust reference is hereby made with the same effect as though recited at length herein; for the description of the property mortgaged; the nature and extent of the security; the rights of the holders; the terms and conditions upon which the bonds are issued, held and secured; and may before their fixed maturities be declared at once due and payable; and the manner of prepayment before maturity".

Some authorities have held that the above references do not incorporate into the bonds the entire contents of the trust indenture but only such portions thereof relating to the matters specified in such legend of incorporation. It is the opinion of the Referee that in this particular case if the reference to incorporation had incorporated the entire contents of the trust indenture into the bonds the situation would not have been materially changed or affected. If the bank had undertaken to examine the trust indenture it would have learned that there was an agreement between the parties for the maintenance of a trust fund of Thirty Thousand ($30,-000.00) Nevertheless, the bonds were duly and fully executed, authenticated and issued, and it is the opinion of the Trustee that notice of the particular clause as to the trust or reserve could not be notice to the banks of a defect without an examination of the parties or of the records to disclose whether or not the particular contention had been complied with at the time the bonds were tendered for collateral security to the bank, and, in addition thereto, an examination of the later clause permitting the Trustee, its officers, agents, or stockholders to own, handle and deal in said bonds without question would have vitiated any notice which the bank might be expected to acquire of the Thirty Thousand ($30,000.00) Dollars reserve provision.

It Is the Opinion of the Trustee,

First, That the deposit of said bonds with the banks as collateral aforesaid was not in violation of the Uniform Fiduciaries Act, Statute 112, R. S. Wisconsin.

Second, That the bonds in question are negotiable instruments; and

Third, That the bonds as negotiable instruments were complete and regular upon the face; that the bank became the holder before maturity and without notice of dishonor; that the bank took the bonds in good faith and for value; that at the time of cancellation the bank had no notice of deformity or defect in title and was taken in the usual course of business.

Wherefore, It Is Ordered, that the cross petition of Kalt Zimmers Manufacturing Company objecting to the permission of the Court to the Marine National Exchange Bank, of Milwaukee, Wisconsin, to offer for sale and sell the bonds of the Kalt Zimmers Manufacturing Company under the terms and conditions of its collateral note be denied and that the Marine National Exchange Bank, aforesaid, be authorized and empowered to offer for sale and sell the said bonds of Kalt Zimmers Manufacturing Company held by it as collateral to secure promissory notes of Hackett, Hoff & Thier-

38   mann, Inc., in accordance with the terms and provisions of said collateral deposit; and

It Is Further Ordered, that the cross petition of Kalt Zimmers Manufacturing Company objecting to the permission of the Court to the West Side Bank, of Milwaukee, Wisconsin, to offer for sale and sell the bonds of the Kalt Zimmers Manufacturing Company under the terms and conditions of its collateral note be denied and that the West Side Bank, aforesaid, be authorized and empowered to offer for sale and sell the said bonds of Kalt Zimmers Manufacturing Company held by it as collateral to secure promissory notes of Hackett, Hoff & Thiermann, Inc., in accordance with the terms and provisions of said collateral deposit.

Dated at Racine, Wisconsin, March 11, 1933.

MILTON J. KNOBLOCK
Referee in Bankruptcy.

Endorsed: "Filed March 11, Milton Knoblock, Referee."

39 PETITION OF KALT-ZIMMERS MANUFACTUR-
ING CO. for a review of the Referee's Order of March
11, 1933, filed as follows:

* * (Caption) * *

And now comes your petitioner herein, the Kalt-Zimmers
Manufacturing Company, a Wisconsin corporation, and respectfully represents and shows to this honorable court that
heretofore, to-wit, on or about the 15th day of August, A. D.
1929, it made, executed, and delivered its six per cent. (6%)
Refunding First Mortgage or deed of trust to Hackett, Hoff
& Thiermann, Inc., the above named bankrupt corporation,
as trustee, to secure an issue of One Hundred Fifteen Thousand dollars ($115,000.00) of its serially maturing bonds.
40   That under the terms of said mortgage or deed of trust
the said Hackett, Hoff & Thiermann, Inc., as trustee, was
to hold in trust for your petitioner all of said bonds and the
proceeds thereof for the purpose of paying and retiring the
First Mortgage bond issue when the same became due and
payable, and paying for certain improvements upon the
premises of your petitioner. (See pages 9 and 10 of the deed
of trust.)

Your petitioner further shows that the said Hackett, Hoff
& Thiermann, Inc., the bankrupt herein, in violation of said
trust pledged with other collateral as security to its personal loans at the Marine National Exchange Bank of Milwaukee, Wisconsin, Six Thousand dollars ($6,000.00) par
value of the said bonds so issued by your petitioner, and likewise pledged with other collateral as security to its personal
loans at the West Side Bank of Milwaukee, Wisconsin,
Eighty-five Hundred dollars ($8500.00) par value of the said
bonds so issued by your petitioner.

Your petitioner further shows that said Hackett, Hoff &
Thiermann, Inc., was adjudicated a bankrupt on the 6th day
of June, 1931, and that thereafter M. H. Grossman, Esq.,
was duly elected trustee in bankruptcy of said Hackett, Hoff
& Thiermann, Inc., bankrupt, qualified as such trustee and is
now the duly elected, qualified, and acting trustee in bankruptcy of said bankrupt.

That thereafter and on or about the 23d day of September,
1931, the Marine National Exchange Bank duly filed its peti-

tion in the above named bankruptcy proceedings, setting forth that the above named bankrupt was indebted to said Marine National Exchange Bank in the sum of Eighty-seven Thousand Seven Hundred Sixty-seven and 82/100 dollars ($87,767.82) together with interest from March 31, 1931, and in said petition prayed leave to sell and dispose of the

41 security which it held as collateral to said obligations, among which collateral was Six Thousand dollars ($6,000.00) par value of the said Refunding First Mortgage Gold bonds issued by your petitioner and which were a part of the bonds so held in trust by said bankrupt under the terms of the trust deed herein referred to; and the West Side Bank likewise duly filed its petition in the same manner, likewise setting forth the obligations of said bankrupt to it, and likewise praying leave to sell and dispose of the security which was collateralized to said loan, among which collateral was Eighty-five hundred dollars ($8500.00) par value of the said Refunding First Mortgage Gold bonds issued by your petitioner and which were a part of the bonds to be held in trust by said bankrupt under the terms of the said trust deed herein referred to.

Your petitioner further shows that thereafter and in due time it did file its answer and cross petition to the said petitions of the Marine National Exchange Bank and the West Side Bank herein referred to, in which answers and cross petitions this petitioner set forth the provisions of the bond and the provisions of the trust indenture, asserting your petitioner's right to a return to it of the bonds so sought to be sold by the said Marine National Exchange Bank and the West Side Bank and denying said banks and said bankrupt's trustee the right to hold or sell said bonds.

Your petitioner further shows that thereafter and pursuant to a ruling of the Honorable Referee in Bankruptcy, the said petitioners, Marine National Exchange Bank and West Side Bank, were duly ruled to answer the said cross petitions of your petitioner herein, and that said Marine National Exchange Bank and said West Side Bank duly filed their

42 respective answers to the cross petition of your petitioner filed in this proceeding, to which answers is attached photostatic copy of one of the bonds issued by your petitioner and held by said Marine National Exchange Bank of Milwaukee and said West Side Bank, all of the bonds so held by said Marine National Exchange Bank and said West

Side Bank being identical in form except as to numbers and denominations, and which said bonds incorporated the provisions of said trust deed as to said trust as a part of said bonds.

Your petitioner further shows that thereafter and in due time M. H. Grossman as trustee in bankruptcy of the above named bankrupt duly served and filed his answer to the cross petitions of your petitioner herein.

Your petitioner further shows that thereafter and pursuant to notice to all parties in interest given by Milton J. Knobloch, Esq., Referee in Bankruptcy, said matter upon the petition of the Marine National Exchange Bank and upon the petition of the West Side Bank, the answers and cross petitions of your petitioner, the answers to the cross petition of your petitioner by the Marine National Exchange Bank and the West Side Bank and M. H. Grossman, Esq., trustee in bankruptcy, came on to be heard before the said Milton J. Knobloch, Referee in Bankruptcy commencing on October 17, 1932, and extending over various adjourned dates, and on the 11th day of March, 1933, the said Milton J. Knobloch, Referee in Bankruptcy, made and entered an order denying the rights, claims, by your petitioner herein under its cross petitions filed in the above entitled matter, and granting leave to

the Marine National Exchange Bank of Milwaukee and 43 the West Side Bank to offer for sale and sell the bonds of the Kalt-Zimmers Manufacturing Company pledged to said banks as herein set forth and denying your petitioner to any relief therefrom.

Your petitioner further respectfully shows that said order so entered by said Referee in Bankruptcy manifests error and prejudice to the substantial rights of your petitioner in that said Referee in Bankruptcy held that the pledging of said bonds by Hackett, Hoff & Thiermann, Inc., the above named bankrupt was valid and enforceable; that said bonds were negotiable and that the trust and escrow created under the trust deed pursuant to which said bonds were issued was not effective in respect to the bonds pledged by said bankrupt to the said Marine National Exchange Bank and West Side Bank as herein set forth and that the bank became the holder in due course and had no notice of defect of title. That the order so entered by said Referee in Bankruptcy manifests error and prejudice to the substantial rights of your petitioner in that said Referee did not hold that said bonds so pledged as collateral security by the above named bankrupt to said respective banks were taken by said bank with notice of defect in title and not in the usual course of business, and that the pledging of said bonds with the said banks as collateral was in violation of the Uniform Fiduciary's Act, Chapt. 112, Revised Statutes of Wisconsin, and a breach of trust known to said banks and that said bonds in question are non-negotiable.

Wherefore Your petitioner, feeling aggrieved because of said order of March 11, 1933, prays that the same be re-
44   viewed as provided in the Bankruptcy Law of 1898 and the amendments thereto and the general orders made in pursuance thereof.

Dated at Milwaukee, Wisconsin, this 18th day of March, 1933.

Kalt-Zimmers Manufacturing Company
By Ogarita I. Casper,
President.

United States of America, ⎫
State of Wisconsin,   ⎬ ss.
Milwaukee County.   ⎭

OGARITA CASPER, being first duly sworn, on oath deposes and says that she is the President of the above and foregoing corporation, Kalt-Zimmers Manufacturing Company; that she has read the above and foregoing petition and that the same is true to the best of her knowledge, information and belief; that she makes this vertification for and on behalf of said corporation and is authorized so to do.

Ogarita I. Casper.

Subscribed and sworn to before me this 18th day of March, A. D. 1933.

Florence Buck,
Notary Public, Milwaukee Co., Wis.

(Seal)

My commission expires June 30, 1935.

Endorsed: "Filed March 20, 1933 Milton J. Knoblock, Referee"

45   June 15, 1933—MEMORANDUM OPINION of Hon. ^{Filed J} ^{1938.}
F. A. Geiger, District Judge, relating to said contro-
versy, filed as follows:

*   *   (Caption)   *   *

Memorandum.

The two banks, Marine National Exchange Bank and West
Side Bank, are in possession of bonds pledged to them respectively by the bankrupt to secure personal loans. The
question at issue is the right of the banks to hold them by
virtue of the pledge.

Apparently, the petitioning banks assume that if the bonds
are negotiable the question tendered by Kalt-Zimmers Manufacturing Company must be answered in the negative.

My consideration of the matter leads me to reject the conclusion, even if the assumption be granted. By that is meant
that even if the bonds be negotiable in form and in fact, it
does not follow that the bankrupt, because of that fact alone,
could validly negotiate them in any and in every way.
Plainly, inquiry respecting the bankrupt's real relationship
to such bonds—known to or knowable by a transferee—cannot be foreclosed by the mere fact of their general negotiable

character, even if there be added general good faith,
46   value given on transfer and claimed ordinary course at-
tending the transfer. Therefore, it has seemed to me
that proof of some kind bearing upon the bankrupt's real relationship thereto as affecting claimed rightful negotiation,
was receivable to consider and determine the latter as a basic
inquiry. Whether we term the relationship as a real estate
mortgage trust, or something else, and include the somewhat
general and at times vague idea of "underwriting", we re-
cur to the necessity of inquiry respecting the bankrupt's re-
lation to these bonds; and, if found to be fiduciary, whether
knowledge thereof, is chargeable to the petitioning bankers.
This basic inquiry must start with an examination of the
bonds and their securing mortgage. It may be conceded that
upon such examination there is disclosed a power of the
bankrupt trustee to "negotiate" and "sell" the bonds for
some purpose. It may be particularly further conceded that
if the bankrupt either owned the bonds in its individual right;
or, if not, it could sell them in its capacity as trustee pursu-

ant to power granted. In either event, purchase could be
made without peril. The fact of ownership, whether it be
known or unknown to the purchaser, would control in the one,
as would the undoubted trust power to sell, in the other. The
purchaser would be protected. The trust power for that purpose being adequately granted alone suffices for purposes of
sale.

Therefore the inquiry may assume this form: Do the bonds
and their securing mortgage—including also the underwriting agreement—on their face disclose a limitation on power
of disposition of such bonds? This, it may be true, is merely
another form of stating our earlier inquiry respecting
47 the bankrupt's relationship. It would seem manifest
that when bonds which are held, that is, in the possession
of one seeking to dispose of them, refer to the latter as a
"trustee" under a "mortgage or deed of trust" to which
deed "reference is hereby made with the same effect as
though recited at length herein" for (1) the description of
the property mortgaged, (2) the nature and extent of the security, (3) the rights of the holders of the bonds, and (4) the
"terms and conditions upon which the said bonds are issued,
held and secured", the purpose of the recital and reference
is entirely clear. As was suggested upon oral argument, the
tender of such a bond by its holder or bearer, to any one,
hardly left the latter in a position to refuse to see what was
on its face, or to fail or refuse to inquire what it all meant
with respect to issuance, holding, or security; or with respect to the power to negotiate or sell. In the case before
us, the emphasis arises out of the fact that, upon such face
of the bond (and its reference), the herein bankrupt trustee
is shown to have other than a mere individual relationship.
I believe that the duty was cast upon the one to whom they
tendered, no matter how clearly their negotiability in case
of attempted transfer in execution of a fiduciary power, or
negotiation by sale in case of individual ownership, may otherwise appear from the instrument; that is to say: the fact
of negotiability within limited range is not the sole determiner of a right of a trustee to transfer property once it appears clearly that an individual, and not a trust purpose is
sought to be carried out. Therefore, conceding that if
48 the bonds had a trust status they could be sold in execution of trust powers, they are still left outside of the
trust or any of its powers when it appears there is a non-

trust purpose to "negotiate"; that is, a pledge for the person of the trustee. The infirmity of the banks' position arises out of their knowledge that the bankrupt trustee was tendering the bonds for its personal benefit. In my judgment such infirmity is declared upon principles of trust powers—or as Justice Story put it—in the "stubborn rule of equity" forbidding trustees (and all who know of the trust) from dealing in trust property for the personal benefit of the former. And I do not believe the negotiable instruments law, nor the uniform acts passed by the states, override or impair that principle. The case of *Pollard* v. *Tobin,* decided by the supreme court of Wisconsin, does not, and in my judgment cannot preclude the application and enforcement of such principle in the federal courts. The uniformity here is not met by the circumstance that the bonds are payable to "bearer", but as I conceive, it is created by the facts known to the transferee (1) that the bankrupt was a "bearer"; in trust, and, (2) transferred, by way of pledge for his personal benefit in defiance of the trust. Those facts, within the principle of equity relied upon, preclude the right of transferees to assert that they chose to ignore them or that they ignored them in good faith, or for value, or in due course. And with great respect,

I cannot accept the decision in the Pollard case as justifying the transfers here challenged.
49

An order may be entered reversing the decision of the referee.

F. A. GEIGER,
District Judge.

Endorsed: "Filed June 15, 1933 B. H. Westfahl, Clerk"

50   And afterwards, to-wit: on the 134th day of said
Term, to-wit: on the 15th day of June, A. D. 1933, the following proceedings were had to-wit:

* * (Caption) * *

The Certificate of the Referee for review of an order made by him on March 11, 1933, granting petitions of Marine National Exchange Bank of Milwaukee, and West Side Bank of Milwaukee, for authority to sell certain securities held by them to secure a collateral note of the bankrupt, having been heretofore argued and submitted; on consideration thereof

It Is Ordered by the Court that said order of the Referee be and hereby is reversed.

Further Ordered that the record be returned to the Referee for further proceedings.

Witness the Honorable Ferdinand A. Geiger, Judge of the said Court, and the seal thereof, at Milwaukee, in said District, on the 15th day of June, A. D. 1933.

(Signed) B. H. WESTFAHL,
(L. S.) *Clerk.*

Endorsed: "Filed June 15, 1933 B. H. Westfahl, Clerk"

July 12,   51   July 12, 1933.—PETITION FOR APPEAL AND ORDER ALLOWING APPEAL, filed as follows:

* * (Caption) * *

Petition for Appeal to Circuit Court of Appeals.

To the Honorable Judge of the United States District Court for the Eastern District of Wisconsin:

Your petitioners, Marine National Exchange Bank of Milwaukee, and West Side Bank, conceiving themselves aggrieved by the certain order entered on the 15th day of June, 1933, in the above entitled proceeding reversing an order, entered by the Honorable Milton J. Knoblock, Referee in Bankruptcy, dated the 11th day of March, 1933, which said order granted the petitions of said Marine National Exchange Bank of Milwaukee and West Side Bank to offer for sale and sell certain bonds of the Kalt-Zimmers Manufacturing Company, held by them as collateral, and dismissing the cross petitions of said Kalt-Zimmers Manufacturing Company objecting to such sale, do hereby petition for an appeal from the said order to the United States Circuit Court of Appeals for the Seventh Circuit, and pray that their appeal may be allowed, and that a citation may be granted directed to Kalt-Zimmers Manufacturing Company and to M. H. Grossman, Esq., Trustee in Bankruptcy, commanding them to appear before the United States Circuit Court of Appeals for the Seventh Circuit to do and receive that which may pertain to justice, to be done in the premises, and that a transcript of the record and the evidence in said proceeding, duly authenticated,

52 may be transmitted to the United States Circuit Court of Appeals for the Seventh Circuit.

> MARINE NATIONAL EXCHANGE BANK OF
> MILWAUKEE,
> By LEON E. KAUMHEIMER and
> DOUGLASS VAN DYKE,
> *Its Attorneys.*
> WEST SIDE BANK,
> By GEO. A. AFFELDT,
> *Its Attorney.*

The foregoing appeal of Marine National Exchange Bank of Milwaukee and West Side Bank is hereby allowed, and the amount of the bond to be filed as security for the payment of costs is fixed at the sum of Two Hundred Fifty Dollars ($250.00).

Dated this 12th day of July, A. D. 1933.

> F. A. GEIGER,
> *United States District Judge.*

Endorsed: "Filed July 12, 1933　B. H. Westfahl, Clerk"

53　　　　* * (Caption) * *　　　　Filed 193£

ASSIGNMENT OF ERRORS.

Now comes Marine National Exchange Bank of Milwaukee by Leon E. Kaumheimer, Esq., and Douglass Van Dyke, Esq., its attorneys, and West Side Bank by George A. Affeldt, Esq., its attorney, and file the following assignment of errors, upon which they will rely in the prosecution of an appeal, herewith petitioned for in said cause, from an order made and entered in the above entitled matter on the 15th day of June, A. D. 1933, by the Honorable Ferdinand A. Geiger, Judge of said Court:

1. The United States District Court for the Eastern District of Wisconsin erred in holding (contrary to the findings of the Referee in Bankruptcy) that the Marine National Exchange Bank of Milwaukee and West Side Bank had knowledge, at the time of the pledge, that the bonds pledged to them were held by Hackett, Hoff & Thiermann, Inc., the pledgor, in a trust or fiduciary capacity for Kalt-Zimmers Manufacturing Company, and that the pledge thereof constituted a breach of such trust.

2. The United States District Court for the Eastern District of Wisconsin erred in concluding (contrary to the findings of the Referee in Bankruptcy) that the Marine National Exchange Bank of Milwaukee and West Side Bank were, at the time of the pledge notwithstanding the provisions of section 116.61 of the Wisconsin Statutes of 1931, chargeable with knowledge that the bonds pledged were held by Hackett, Hoff & Thiermann, Inc., the pledgor, in a trust or fiduciary capacity for Kalt-Zimmers Manufacturing Company, and that the pledge thereof constituted a breach of such trust, and that the pledgee acted in bad faith.

3. The United States District Court for the Eastern District of Wisconsin erred in holding (contrary to the conclusion of the Referee in Bankruptcy) that the Marine National Exchange Bank of Milwaukee and West Side Bank acquired no title to the bonds pledged for the reason that said banks had actual knowledge or were chargeable with knowledge that the bonds were held by Hackett, Hoff & Thiermann, Inc., the pledgor, in a trust or fiduciary capacity for Kalt-Zimmers Manufacturing Company, and that the pledge thereof constituted a breach of such trust.

4. If the United States District Court for the Eastern District of Wisconsin in its opinion held that the bonds of Kalt-Zimmers Manufacturing Company were non-negotiable instruments (contrary to the conclusion of the Referee in Bankruptcy), it erred in so holding.

5. If the United States District Court for the Eastern District of Wisconsin in its opinion held (contrary to the conclusion of the Referee in Bankruptcy) that the deposit of the bonds of the Kalt-Zimmers Manufacturing Company by Hackett, Hoff & Thiermann, Inc., as collateral for loans made

by the Marine National Exchange Bank of Milwaukee and West Side Bank, was in violation of the Uniform Fiduciaries Act, Chapter 112, Wisconsin Statutes of 1931, it erred in so holding.

6. The United States District Court for the Eastern District of Wisconsin erred in not granting the petition of the Marine National Exchange Bank of Milwaukee for authority to sell bonds numbered 100, 113 and 116 of the Kalt-Zimmers Manufacturing Company held by it as collateral security, and the petition of the West Side Bank for authority to sell bonds numbered 62, 66, 72, 73 and 74 of the Kalt-Zimmers Manufacturing Company held by it as collateral security 55 (said bonds having been regularly sold by Hackett, Hoff & Thiermann, Inc., and subsequently re-purchased by it before the pledge thereof), and in not denying the cross-petitions of Kalt-Zimmers Manufacturing Company for the delivery of said bonds to the Trustee in Bankruptcy.

7. The United States District Court for the Eastern District of Wisconsin erred in denying the petitions of the Marine National Exchange Bank of Milwaukee and the West Side Bank for authority to sell the bonds of Kalt-Zimmers Manufacturing Company, held by them as collateral security.

8. The United States District Court for the Eastern District of Wisconsin erred in not dismissing the cross-petitions of Kalt-Zimmers Manufacturing Company for an order requiring said Marine National Exchange Bank of Milwaukee and said West Side Bank to deliver to the Trustee in Bankruptcy the bonds of Kalt-Zimmers Manufacturing Company held by them as collateral security.

9. The United States District Court for the Eastern District of Wisconsin erred in reversing the order of Honorable Milton J. Knoblock, Referee in Bankruptcy, dated the 11th day of March, 1933.

Wherefore, the appellants, Marine National Exchange Bank of Milwaukee and West Side Bank, pray that said order of the Honorable Ferdinand A. Geiger, District Judge, dated the 15th day of June, 1933, be reversed, and that said United States District Court for the Eastern District of Wisconsin be directed to vacate said order and to enter an order affirming the order of the Honorable Milton J. Knoblock, Referee in Bankruptcy, dated the 11th day of March, 1933.

Dated at Milwaukee, Wisconsin, this 10th day of July,
A. D. 1933.

> Leon E. Kaumheimer,
> Douglass Van Dyke,
> *Attorneys for appellant, Marine National Exchange Bank of Milwaukee.*
>
> George A. Affeldt,
> *Attorney for appellant, West Side Bank.*

56   (Endorsed) * * (Caption) * * Assignment of
Errors Filed Jul 12 1933 B. H. Westfahl, Clerk.

18,   57   * * (Caption) * *

BOND ON APPEAL.

Know All Men by These Presents: That we, Marine National Exchange Bank of Milwaukee and West Side Bank, as principals, and Fidelity and Deposit Company of Maryland, as surety, are held and firmly bound unto the above named Kalt-Zimmer Manufacturing Company and E. H. Grossman, Esq., Trustee in Bankruptcy, in the sum of Two Hundred Fifty Dollars ($250) for the payment of which well and truly to be made we bind ourselves, our successors and assigns, jointly and severally, firmly by these presents.

Sealed with our seals and dated this 12th day of July, A. D. 1933.

Whereas, an order was entered in the above entitled proceeding in the District Court of the United States for the Eastern District of Wisconsin, on the 12th day of July, 1933, allowing an appeal to the United States Circuit Court of Appeals for the Seventh Circuit from a certain order by said United States District Court made on the 15th day of June, 1933, wherein Kalt-Zimmers Manufacturing Company was cross-petitioner and Marine National Exchange Bank of Milwaukee and West Side Bank were petitioners; and

Whereas, in said order allowing said appeal it was required that appellants give a bond on appeal in the sum of Two Hundred Fifty Dollars ($250).

58   Now, Therefore, the condition of this obligation is such that if the above named shall prosecute their appeal

to effect and answer all damages and costs if they fail to make said appeal good, then this obligation shall be void, otherwise the same shall be and remain in full force and virtue.

> MARINE NATIONAL EXCHANGE BANK OF
> MILWAUKEE,
> By G. W. AUGUSTYN   (Seal)
> *President.*

Attest:
 G. D. PRENTICE,
  Cashier.
Signed, sealed and delivered
 in the presence of:
  ISABELLE M. HEGY
  H. H. VAN MALE

> WEST SIDE BANK,
> By CHAS. J. KUHNMUENCH (Seal)
> *President.*

Attest:
 WM. P. BACKES,
  Cashier.
 FRED RISTOW, JR.
 HENRY J. FARBER

> FIDELITY AND DEPOSIT COMPANY OF
> MARYLAND,
> By WM. M. WOLFF   (Seal)
> *Attorney in Fact.*

 K. L. LOEW
 HAZEL CLEMICK

The above bond is approved as to form and sufficiency this 13th day of July, A. D. 1933.

> F. A. GEIGER,
> *District Judge.*

Endorsed: "Filed July 13, 1933 B. H. Westfahl, Clerk"

18, 101   * * (Caption) * *

PRAECIPE FOR RECORD.

To: Honorable B. H. Westfahl, Clerk of the United States District Court, for the Eastern District of Wisconsin:

You are hereby requested to make a transcript of record to be filed in the United States Circuit Court of Appeals for the Seventh Circuit, pursuant to an appeal allowed in the above entitled cause, and to include in such transcript of record the following, and no other papers and exhibits, to-wit:

1. The petition of the Marine National Exchange Bank of Milwaukee for authority to sell collateral security.

2. Answer and cross-petition of Kalt-Zimmers Manufacturing Company to the petition of the Marine National Exchange Bank of Milwaukee.

3. Answer of the Marine National Exchange Bank of Milwaukee to the cross-petition of the Kalt-Zimmers Manufacturing Company.

4. Answer of M. H. Grossman, Trustee in Bankruptcy, to the cross-petition of Kalt-Zimmers Manufacturing Company.

5. Petition of the West Side Bank for the authority to sell collateral security.

6. Answer and cross-petition of Kalt-Zimmers Manufacturing Company to the petition of the West Side Bank.

7. Answer of the West Side Bank to the cross-petition of the Kalt-Zimmers Manufacturing Company.

102   8. Referee's Findings and Order dated March 11, 1933, upon the above controversy.

9. Petition of Kalt-Zimmers Manufacturing Company for a review of the Referee's Order of March 11, 1933.

10. Certificate of Honorable Wilton J. Knoblock, Referee in Bankruptcy, certifying the foregoing controversy to the District Court of the United States for the Eastern District of Wisconsin.

11. Memorandum Opinion of Honorable Ferdinand A. Geiger, District Judge, relating to said controversy.

12. Order of the District Court of the United States for the Eastern District of Wisconsin, dated the 15th day of June, A. D. 1933.

13. Petition for appeal and order allowing appeal.

14. Assignment of errors and prayer for reversal.

15. Cost bond on appeal with approval thereof.

16. Statement of the evidence, including order allowing the same.

17. Citation with proof of service.

18. Praecipe.

19. Certificate of Clerk of the United States District Court for the Eastern District of Wisconsin.

Dated at Milwaukee, Wisconsin, this 18th day of July, A. D. 1933.

> LEON C. KAUMHEIMER,
> DOUGLASS VAN DYKE,
> *Attorneys for appellant, Marine National Exchange Bank of Milwaukee.*
>
> GEORGE A. AFFELDT,
> *Attorney for appellant, West Side Bank.*

Approved this .... day of July, A. D. 1933.

District Judge.

Endorsed: "Filed July 18, 1933 B. H. Westfahl, Clerk"

103   CERTIFICATE OF CLERK.

United States of America,   ⎰
Eastern District of Wisconsin. ⎱ ss:

I, B. H. Westfahl, Clerk of the District Court of the United States of America for the Eastern District of Wisconsin, do hereby certify that I have compared the writings annexed to this Certificate, and that they are true copies of the record of proceedings and other papers, together with the original condensed statement of evidence, assignment of errors and citation on appeal of Marine National Exchange Bank of Milwaukee and West Side Bank from the order dated June 15, 1933, in the matter of Hackett, Hoff & Thiermann, Inc., bankrupt.

In Testimony Whereof, I have hereunto set my hand, and duly affixed the seal of said Court at the City of Milwaukee, in said District this 2nd day of August, in the year of our Lord, one thousand nine hundred thirty-three, and of the Independence of the United States, the 158th.

> B. H. WESTFAHL,
> *Clerk.*

(Seal)

99   *   *   (Caption)   *   *

CITATION ON APPEAL.

United States
  of America } ss.

The President of the United States of America, to Kalt-Zimmers Manufacturing Company and M. H. Grossmann, Esq., Trustee in Bankruptcy:

You, and each of you, are hereby admonished to appear in the United States Circuit Court of Appeals for the Seventh Circuit in the City of Chicago, State of Illinois, on the 11th day of August, A. D. 1933, pursuant to an appeal duly obtained and filed in the Clerk's office in the United States District Court for the Eastern District of Wisconsin, wherein you are appellees and Marine National Exchange Bank of Milwaukee and West Side Bank are appellants, to show cause, if any there be, why the order in said appeal mentioned should not be reversed and corrected, and why speedy justice should not be done to the parties in that behalf, and to do and receive that which may appertain to justice to be done in the premises.

Witness, the Honorable Ferdinand A. Geiger, United States District Judge, for the Eastern District of Wisconsin, on the 12 day of July, in the year of our Lord, One Thousand Nine Hundred Thirty-three.

           F. A. GEIGER,
(Seal)   *United States District Judge.*

100   (Endorsed)   *   *   (Caption)   *   *   Citation on Appeal. Due service on behalf of Kalt-Zimmers Manufacturing Company of the within citation on appeal admitted this 14th day of July, 1933. Fish, Marshutz & Hoffman, Attorneys for Kalt-Zimmers Mfg. Company Due service on behalf of Kalt-Zimmers Manufacturing Company of the within citation on appeal admitted this 14th day of July, 1933. Bender, Trump, McIntyre & Freeman, Attorneys for M. H. Grossman, Trustee in Bankruptcy. Filed July 14 1933 at 4 o'clock P. M. B. H. Westfahl, Clerk.

UNITED STATES CIRCUIT COURT OF APPEALS

For the Seventh Circuit.

———

I, Frederick G. Campbell, Clerk of the United States Circuit Court of Appeals for the Seventh Circuit, do hereby certify that the foregoing printed pages, numbered from 1 to 88, inclusive, contain a true copy of the printed record, printed under my supervision and filed on the fifth day of September, 1933, and used and considered at the hearing on the determination of the following entitled cause:

In the Matter of Hackett, Hoff & Thiermann, Inc., Bankrupt.

———

Marine National Exchange Bank of Milwaukee and West Side Bank,

Appellants,

vs.

Kalt-Zimmers Manufacturing Company and M. H. Grossmann, Trustee in Bankruptcy,

Appellees,

No. 5048, October Term, 1933, as the same remains upon the files and records of the United States Circuit Court of Appeals for the Seventh Circuit.

In Testimony Whereof I hereunto subscribe my name and affix the seal of said United States Circuit Court of Appeals for the Seventh Circuit, at the City of Chicago, this 8th day of June, A. D. 1934.

FREDERICK G. CAMPBELL,

(Seal)   *Clerk of the United States Circuit Court of Appeals for the Seventh Circuit.*

At a regular term of the United States Circuit Court of Appeals for the Seventh Circuit begun and held in the United States Court Room in the City of Chicago, in said Seventh Circuit, on the fourth day of October, 1932, of the October Term, in the year of our Lord one thousand nine hundred and thirty-two, and of our Independence the one hundred and fifty-seventh.

In the Matter of Hackett, Hoff & Thiermann, Inc., Bankrupt.

Marine National Exchange Bank of Milwaukee and West Side Bank,
Appellants,

5048   *vs.*

Kalt-Zimmers Manufacturing Company and M. H. Grossman, Trustee in Bankruptcy,
Appellees.

Appeal from the District Court of the United States for the Eastern District of Wisconsin.

And afterwards, to-wit: On the seventh day of August, 1933, there was filed in the office of the Clerk of this Court, an appearance of counsel for appellees, which said appearance is in the words and figures following, to-wit:

UNITED STATES CIRCUIT COURT OF APPEALS

For the Seventh Circuit.

No. 5048.   October Term, 1932.

In the Matter of Hackett, Hoff & Thiermann, Inc., Bankrupt.

Marine National Exchange Bank of Milwaukee, *et al.,*
Appellants,

vs.

Kalt-Zimmers Manufacturing Company, *et al.,*
Appellees.

The Clerk will enter our appearance as counsel for appellees.

I. A. FISH,
J. H. MARSHUTZ,
G. R. HOFFMAN,
Wells Building,
Milwaukee, Wisconsin.

Endorsed: Filed August 7, 1933. Frederick G. Campbell, Clerk.

And afterwards, to-wit: On the tenth day of August, 1933, there was filed in the office of the clerk of this Court, an appearance of counsel for appellant, which said appearance is in the words and figures following, to-wit:

UNITED STATES CIRCUIT COURT OF APPEALS

For the Seventh Circuit.

No. 5048.   October Term, 1932.

In the Matter of Hackett, Hoff & Thiermann, Inc., Bankrupt.

Marine National Exchange Bank of Milwaukee, *et al.,*
Appellants,

vs.

Kalt-Zimmers Manufacturing Company, *et al.,*
Appellees.

The clerk will enter my appearance as counsel for appellant.

LEON E. KAUMHEIMER,
Wells Building,
Milwaukee, Wisconsin.

Endorsed: Filed August 10, 1933. Frederick G. Campbell, Clerk.

At a regular term of the United States Circuit Court of Appeals for the Seventh Circuit begun and held in the United States Court Room in the City of Chicago, in said Seventh Circuit, on the third day of October, 1933, of the October Term, in the year of our Lord one thousand nine hundred and thirty-three, and of our Independence the one hundred and fifty-eighth.

And afterwards, to-wit: On the ninth day of January, 1934, the following further proceedings were had and entered of record, to-wit:

Tuesday, January 9, 1934.

Court met pursuant to adjournment and was opened by proclamation.

Before:

Hon. Samuel Alschuler, Circuit Judge.
Hon. Evan A. Evans, Circuit Judge.
Hon. William M. Sparks, Circuit Judge.

In the Matter of Hackett, Hoff & Thiermann, Inc., Bankrupt.

———

Marine National Exchange Bank of Milwaukee, *et al.*,
5048   *vs.*
Kalt-Zimmers Manufacturing Company, *et al.*

Appeal from the District Court of the United States for the Eastern District of Wisconsin.

It is ordered by the Court that this cause be, and the same is hereby set down for hearing on February 1, 1934.

———

And afterwards, to-wit: On the first day of February, 1934, the following further proceedings were had and entered of record, to-wit:

Thursday, February 1, 1934.

Court met pursuant to adjournment and was opened by proclamation.

Before:

Hon. Evan A. Evans, Circuit Judge.
Hon. William M. Sparks, Circuit Judge.
Hon. Louis FitzHenry, Circuit Judge.

In the Matter of Hackett, Hoff & Thiermann, Inc., Bankrupt.

———

Marine National Exchange Bank of Milwaukee, *et al.*,
5048   *vs.*
Kalt-Zimmers Manufacturing Company, *et al.*

Appeal from the District Court of the United States for the Eastern District of Wisconsin.

Now this day come the parties by their counsel and this cause now comes on to be heard on the printed record and briefs of counsel and on oral arguments by Mr. Leon E. Kaumheimer, and Mr. George Affeld, counsel for appellants, and by Mr. I. A. Fish, counsel for appellee, and the Court having heard the same takes this matter under advisement.

———

And afterwards, to-wit: · On the eighteenth day of April, 1934, there was filed in the office of the Clerk of this Court, the Opinion of the Court, which said Opinion is in the words and figures following, to-wit:

IN THE UNITED STATES CIRCUIT COURT OF APPEALS

For the Seventh Circuit.

———

No. 5048.   October Term, 1933, April Session, 1934.

———

In the Matter of
HACKETT, HOFF and THIERMANN, INC.,
Bankrupt.

———

MARINE NATIONAL EXCHANGE BANK OF MILWAUKEE and WEST SIDE BANK,
Appellants,
vs.
KALT-ZIMMERS MANUFACTURING COMPANY, and M. H. GROSSMAN, Trustee in Bankruptcy,
Appellees.

Appeal from the District Court of the United States for the Eastern District of Wisconsin.

———

April 18, 1934.

———

Before EVANS, SPARKS, and FITZHENRY, *Circuit Judges.*

Appellants, two banks doing business in Milwaukee, Wisconsin, petitioned the referee in bankruptcy of the firm of Hackett, Hoff and Thiermann, Inc., hereafter referred to as the Hackett firm, for permission to sell certain bonds issued by appellee, Kalt-Zimmers Manufacturing Company, hereafter referred to as Kalt-Zimmers. The bonds had been pledged to appellants by the Hackett firm who were the trustees under the trust deed securing the bonds. The referee granted the permission, but his decision was reversed by the District Court.

SPARKS, *Circuit Judge.* Two questions are involved in this appeal: Were the bonds negotiable instruments, and were the banks holders in due course? A negative answer to either question would prevent the banks' recovery and sustain the decision of the District Court.

In August, 1929, Kalt-Zimmers, a manufacturing concern located in Milwaukee, executed and delivered to the Hackett firm, a Wisconsin corporation, as trustee, a deed of trust conveying certain of its property as security for a bond issue of $115,000. The bonds contained the following provision:

> "Said bonds are issued under and secured by a mortgage or deed of trust of even date herewith, duly made, * * to which deed of trust reference is hereby made with the same effect as though recited at length herein, for the description of the property mortgaged, the nature and extent of the security, the rights of the holders of the bonds, and the terms and conditions upon which the said bonds are issued, held, and secured, and may, before their fixed maturities, be declared at once due and payable, and the manner of prepayment before maturity."

The trust deed, after reciting the facts regarding a prior encumbrance of $55,000, of which $35,000 was still outstanding, provided that the trustee should first set aside sufficient bonds of the new issue or the proceeds thereof to satisfy the first mortgage, after which the proceeds of the remainder were to be used in the erection of a building on Kalt-Zimmers' premises, and the balance, if any, was to be at the disposal of Kalt-Zimmers. The bonds secured by the trust deed were to pass by delivery unless registered, and the trustee was given the right to acquire, own and deal in the bonds and coupons with the same rights as if it were not trustee. This trust deed was duly recorded in October, 1929.

The books of account of the Hackett firm with respect to this bond issue showed bonds unsold in the amount of $21,000, and cash on hand in the sum of $25,000. The Hackett firm was adjudicated a bankrupt on June 8, 1931. At that time it was indebted to the Marine Bank in the amount of $87,767, and to the West Side Bank in the amount of $72,019. To secure these sums the bankrupt had from time to time pledged various securities as collateral, including some of the bonds of Kalt-Zimmers. After the adjudication each of the banks filed with the referee a petition for permission to sell these various securities showing that the Marine Bank held Kalt-Zimmers' bonds in the amount of $6000, and the West Side

Bank, $8500. Kalt-Zimmers filed its answer and cross-petition, setting up the facts as to the execution of the trust deed and the issuing of the bonds, alleging failure of consideration for the bonds, denying appellants' title to them, and praying delivery of the bonds to appellees. The answers of the banks to this cross-petition were substantially the same, and alleged that the bonds were negotiable, that the banks became their holders in due course with no notice of any infirmity in the bonds or defect of bankrupt's title, and further that they were delivered by Kalt-Zimmers to the bankrupt who was clothed with apparent authority to transfer and negotiate them.

The District Court did not pass on the question of negotiability, but held that the banks were not holders in due course; that even though the bonds were negotiable, that alone was insufficient to excuse the banks from inquiry concerning the trustee's power to pledge them for what the banks knew was the trustee's personal indebtedness.

Appellants urge that this ruling contravenes a recent decision of the Supreme Court of Wisconsin, *Pollard* v. *Tobin*, ... Wis. ...., 247 N. W. 453. That decision involved the identical question now under consideration, arising out of a transaction between the same bankrupt and another bank, in which there were pledged under similar circumstances, bonds practically identical in form and terms with the bonds herein involved. There the court held that the bonds were negotiable, and that the bank was a holder in due course, although the evidence showed that they had been accepted as collateral after one of the members of the bankrupt pledgor had committed suicide, and after the bank had made inquiry of another bank in which the bankrupt had its principal checking account as to the effect of the suicide upon the firm's solvency. The bank apparently had been satisfied with the answer of the other bank that in fact the bankrupt was put in a stronger position by reason of the fact that it had carried insurance upon the deceased member, and that the bankrupt was solvent anyway. We would have supposed that under those facts the bank accepting the bonds as security for personal loans of the bankrupt would have been held to inquire as to the title of the bankrupt to the bonds, and his right to pledge them, since the bonds showed on their face that the pledgor held them as trustee, and since they referred to the trust deed in which it was recited that the bonds were to be sold by the Hackett firm as soon as possible after delivery. It seems to us that those

facts would have prevented the bank from asserting that it
"had no notice of any defect in the title of the person negotiating" them, and would have necessitated a finding that
the bank had knowledge of such facts that its action in accepting the bonds as a pledge amounted to bad faith under
section 116.61 of the Wisconsin statutes.[1] In the case at bar
we agree with the view of the District Court that "* * the
duty was cast upon the one to whom they tendered, no matter how clearly their negotiability in case of attempted
transfer in execution of a fiduciary power, or negotiation by
sale in case of individual ownership, may otherwise appear
from the instrument; that is to say: the fact of negotiability
within limited range is not the sole determiner of a right of
a trustee to transfer property once it appears clearly that an
individual, and not a trust purpose is sought to be carried
out. * * The infirmity of the bank's position arises out of
their knowledge that the bankrupt trustee was tendering the
bonds for its personal benefit."

The District Court in reaching its conclusion relied on
broad principles of equity forbidding trustees from dealing
in trust property for their own benefit. The plain terms of
the bonds stated that they were trust bonds, and that the
holders' rights thereto were set forth in the deed of trust,
which was made a part of the bonds by reference. Appellants, therefore, could not disregard that notice and inno-
cently accept the bonds as a pledge of security for the trustee's personal debt to appellants, when in fact the trust deed
gave no authority to pledge them in any manner. See *Sanger
v. Farnham*, 220 Mass. 34; *Brovan v. Kyle*, 166 Wis. 347;
Whitford v. *Moehlenpah*, 196 Wis. 10; *Greene v. Greene*, 19
R. I. 619; *Townsend* v. *Wilson*, 77 Conn. 411; *Colonial Trust
Co.* v. *Brown*, 105 Conn. 261. This principle was very clearly
set out in *Jaudon* v. *Duncan*, 15 Wall. 165, which held that the
duty of inquiry was imposed on a lender lending on stocks
where the stock certificates disclosed a trust, and that notice
to the cashier of a bank that the stock pledged was a trust
stock was notice to the bank. The failure to perform that
duty by appellants in the instant case, we think, amounted to
bad faith on their part, as contemplated by section 116.61
of the Wisconsin Statutes. The same principle is supported

---

[1] "SECTION 116.61. To constitute notice of an infirmity in the instrument
or defect in the title of the person negotiating the same, the person to whom
it is negotiated must have had actual knowledge of the infirmity or defect,
or knowledge of such facts that his action in taking the instrument amounted
to bad faith."

·quite generally throughout the states. See *Shaw* v. *Saranac Horsenail Co.*, 144 N. Y. 220; *First National Bank* v. *National Broadway Bank*, 156 N. Y. 459; *Loring* v. *Brodie*, 134 Mass. 453; *Tuttle* v. *First National Bank*, 187 Mass. 533.

In 26 R. C. L. 1223, section 185, it is said:

> "A pledge by a trustee, to secure his own debt, of what is known to be trust property, is prima facie unauthorized, and one taking such security is bound at his peril to ascertain whether the trustee has power to give it. Notice of the existence of a trust is, by all the authorities, held to impose the duty of inquiry as to its character and limitations. * * * So the term trustee in a stock certificate issued to the holder in his name 'as trustee' is sufficient to put persons on inquiry as to the holder's right to pledge them for his own debt, and a pledgee taking them without inquiry does so at his peril. And evidence that stock certificates, issued in the name of one as trustee, and by him transferred in blank, are constantly bought and sold in the market without inquiry, is inadmissible, as varying an established rule of law. (Citing *Shaw* v. *Spencer*, 100 Mass. 382.)"

We do not overlook the fact that the pronouncement just quoted deals with a certificate of stock which was issued in the name of the trustee, and by him transferred, while the bonds in the instant case were payable to bearer. Kalt-Zimmers, however, are relying on more than mere knowledge on the part of appellants that a trust existed. There is the additional fact that appellants knew or should have known the contents of that trust deed and that it gave no authority to pledge the bonds, and we think that under those circumstances appellants accepted the pledges at their peril. If appellants here admitted having read the trust deed prior to accepting the pledges, thus admitting a knowledge of the trustee's lack of power to pledge, we suppose it would not be contended that they accepted the pledge in good faith, merely because the bonds were negotiable. But we think a knowledge of the contents of the trust deed must be imputed to appellants, because they were virtually told by the language of the bonds to read the trust deed in order to ascertain the rights of the trustee as holder.

In *Cordova* v. *Hood*, 84 U. S. 1, Shields had sold and conveyed a tract of land in Texas, with covenants of warranty to Hood, upon receipt of the purchase price. The deed showed that the purchase price was not fully paid, and under the laws of Texas, a vendor's lien enured to the grantor. Shields subsequently assigned Hood's negotiable note, which had been given as part payment of the consideration, to Bartlett. Hood later sold the land to Scroggin and Hanna. Bartlett thereafter was adjudicated a bankrupt and his assignee in bankruptcy, Cordova, filed a bill to enforce the vendor's lien against Scroggin and Hanna, who answered that they were good faith purchasers without notice of any lien. The court, on page 8 of the opinion, said:

"* * The deed from Shields to Hood informed them that the consideration was unpaid. It imposed upon them the duty of inquiring whether it remained unpaid when they were about to make their purchase. Wherever inquiry is a duty, the party bound to make it is affected with knowledge of all which he would have discovered had he performed the duty. Means of knowledge with the duty of using them are, in equity, equivalent to knowledge itself. Had inquiry been made of the vendor, it would easily have been ascertained that a portion of the purchase-money remained unpaid. Inquiry of Hood, the debtor, if any such inquiry was made, was an idle ceremony. The deed pointed to the person from whom purchasers from Hood were bound to seek information."

In the instant case appellants knew the bonds were trust bonds and that the pledgor was the trustee. They further knew, as a matter of law, that the trustee could not pledge the bonds, as security for its personal debts, unless the deed of trust expressly gave that power. The bonds pointed to the trust deed as the source of power from which appellants were bound to seek information on that subject, or they could have acquired the same information had they inquired of Kalt-Zimmers. It is quite true that under the trust deed the trustee had the right to purchase the bonds, and if it had done so, it could have pledged them. But it had not purchased them, and appellants made no inquiry concerning that fact. There were present the means of knowledge and the duty of using them, and as stated in the Hood case, they were equivalent to knowledge itself. If this does not constitute actual knowledge within the meaning of the Hood case, it presents a very strong case of constructive knowledge which in our opinion amounts to bad faith under the Wisconsin statute.

The federal courts are not bound by a decision of a state

court in the interpretation or application of a provision of a uniform law contrary to the weight of authority as established by decisions of other states. *Commercial Bank* v. *Canal Bank,* 239 U. S. 520. We think the decision of the Wisconsin Supreme Court in the Tobin case is contrary to the weight of authority throughout the states. In that case the court was not confronted with ambiguity of statutory terms, nor are we. The language of the statute is quite plain. The question there, as here, is whether appellants had knowledge of such facts that their action in taking the bonds as pledges for the trustee's personal obligations amounted to bad faith. It is true we find no case in which the facts are identical with this or the Tobin case, but the principles of law hereinbefore referred to we think are directly in point and are supported quite generally by the state courts including Wisconsin. Those principles, of course, would not abrogate the plain provisions of the Wisconsin Negotiable Instruments Statute; but we find nothing in that act which seems to be inconsistent with those principles, nor any indication of intention to modify or abrogate them, but on the contrary, the statute seems to reiterate them, for it recognizes a defect in title of a negotiable instrument where it is taken in bad faith.

It is contended by appellants, however, that the trustee purchased the bonds from Kalt-Zimmers. We think that was not the intention of the parties. If that were true there was no occasion for inserting in the trust deed the clause permitting the trustee to sell and purchase the bonds without accounting for the profit. It is also contended by appellants that the preliminary instrument signed by the trustee and Kalt-Zimmers constituted an underwriter's agreement and that an amount equal to the face of the bonds was loaned by the trustee Kalt-Zimmers. This agreement was in the form of a proposal by the Hackett firm, accepted by Kalt-Zimmers, and it contained in general terms the plans, terms, and conditions upon which the bonds should be issued. While it was executed prior to the trust deed and purported to be a proposal for a loan, yet it is quite necessary to consider both the proposal and the trust deed in arriving at the parties' intention as to the character of the entire transaction. When these are thus considered it is apparent that there was no intention to create a loan from the Hackett firm, and if there were such intention in the proposal it was frustrated by the terms of the trust deed which was subsequently executed. It has been held that an underwriter's contract is not an agreement to loan money. *Busch* v. *Stromberg-Carlson Tel. Mfg. Co.*, 217 Fed. 328; *In re Danville Hotel Co.*, 38 F. (2d) 10.

It is quite clear that there was no underwriter's agreement existing between Kalt-Zimmers and the Hackett firm, because there was no agreement on the part of the Hackett firm to take and pay for the bonds which the public did not take. Fletcher's Cyclopedia of Corporations, Vol. I, page 950, defines underwriting as an agreement, made before the shares are brought before the public, that in the event the public does not take all the shares or the number mentioned in the agreement, the underwriters will take the shares which the public does not take. See also Vol. I Cook on Corporations (7th Ed.) par. 14, page 74; *Fraser* v. *Home Telephone and Telegraph Co.*, 91 Wash. 253. The preliminary contract and the trust deed constituted merely an agreement on the part of the Hackett firm to sell Kalt-Zimmers' bonds for a stated commission, and for that purpose it accepted them in trust limited in title by the terms of the trust deed. Whether a valid consideration moved to the trustee from appellants is not now material, because it bargained with them to do a thing which they knew it had no right to do, and for this they can not be held holders in due course.

Decree affirmed.

Endorsed: Filed April 18, 1934. Frederick G. Campbell, Clerk.

And on the same day, to-wit: On the eighteenth day of April, 1934, the following further proceedings were had and entered of record, to-wit:

Wednesday, April 18, 1934.

Court met pursuant to adjournment and was opened by proclamation.

Before:

      Hon. Evan A. Evans, Circuit Judge.
      Hon. William M. Sparks, Circuit Judge.
      Hon. Louis FitzHenry, Circuit Judge.

In the Matter of Hackett, Hoff & Thiermann, Inc., Bankrupt.

Marine National Exchange Bank of Milwaukee, and West Side Bank 5048   *vs.*
Kalt-Zimmers Manufacturing Company and M. H. Grossmann, Trustee in Bankruptcy.

Appeal from the District Court of the United States for the Eastern District of Wisconsin.

This cause came on to be heard on the transcript of the record from the District Court of the United States for the Eastern District of Wisconsin, and was argued by counsel.

On Consideration Whereof: It is now here ordered, adjudged and decreed by this Court that the order or decree of the said District Court in this cause appealed from be, and the same is hereby affirmed with costs.

104

UNITED STATES CIRCUIT COURT OF APPEALS

For the Seventh Circuit.

I, Frederick G. Campbell, Clerk of the United States Circuit Court of Appeals for the Seventh Circuit, do hereby certify that the foregoing printed pages, numbered from 91 to 103, inclusive, contain a true copy of the proceedings had and papers filed (excepting briefs of counsel) in the case of

In the Matter of Hackett, Hoff & Thiermann, Inc., Bankrupt.

Marine National Exchange Bank of Milwaukee and West Side Bank,
Appellants,

vs.

Kalt-Zimmers Manufacturing Company and M. H. Grossmann, Trustee in Bankruptcy,
Appellees,

No. 5048, October Term, 1933, as the same remains upon the files and records of the United States Circuit Court of Appeals for the Seventh Circuit.

In Testimony Whereof I hereunto subscribe my name and affix the seal of said United States Circuit Court of Appeals for the Seventh Circuit, at the City of Chicago, this 8th day of June, A. D. 1934.

FREDERICK G. CAMPBELL,

(Seal) *Clerk of the United States Circuit Court of Appeals for the Seventh Circuit.*

106

[fol. 106] Supreme Court of the United States

Order Allowing Certiorari—Filed October 8, 1934

The petition herein for a writ of certiorari to the United States Circuit Court of Appeals for the Seventh Circuit is granted. And it is further ordered that the duly certified copy of the transcript of the proceedings below which accompanied the petition shall be treated as though filed in response to such writ.

(5514-C)